BURT FRANKLIN: BIBLIOGRAPHY & REFERENCE SERIES 267

THE

WORDSWORTH DICTIONARY

OF

PERSONS AND PLACES

THE

WORDSWORTH DICTIONARY

OF

PERSONS AND PLACES

WITH THE

FAMILIAR QUOTATIONS FROM HIS WORKS
(INCLUDING FULL INDEX)

AND A

CHRONOLOGICALLY-ARRANGED LIST OF
HIS BEST POEMS

BY

J.^{ohn} R. TUTIN

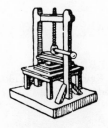

BURT FRANKLIN
NEW YORK

Published by BURT FRANKLIN
235 East 44th St., New York, N.Y. 10017
Originally Published: Hull 1891
Reprinted: 1968
Printed in the U.S.A.

Library of Congress Card Catalog No.: 79-76128
Burt Franklin: Bibliography and Reference Series 267

CONTENTS.

APPENDIX.

PREFACE.

THE deep and reverent study of the works of the classic authors of our country is undoubtedly an important feature of nineteenth-century intellectual life, and a work like the present, it is hoped, may be the means of still further promoting such a study. Concordances to the writings of Shakespeare, Milton, Pope, Cowper, Burns, and Tennyson have been published, but such a useful aid to the study of Wordsworth is still a *desideratum*. The present volume may be taken as an *apology* for a Wordsworth Concordance. Its ground covers some of the more important features of the Poet's work—his numerous allusions to Persons and Places. I have myself long felt the desire for such an aid to the study of the Poet as is now offered, and I put it forth feeling that it would be of real utility to every student and admirer of his works. I have therefore endeavoured to index every description of, or reference to, persons (Contemporary, Historical, Mythical, &c.) named or described in the Poems. The same has been attempted as regards the Places. No other English Poet is so peculiarly associated with locality as is Wordsworth. This latter feature is the more interesting, for wherever he went there has he become associated, and his poems are an index to his travels. Often, too, he has interpreted to us the very heart of the scene, as for example in the following lines on Yarrow :—

> " Meek loveliness is round thee spread,
>   A softness still and holy ;
> The grace of forest charms decayed,
>   And pastoral melancholy."

And the picture is for ever afterwards treasured in
that " mansion for all lovely forms," the human mind.
A glance through the Place-Index section of the
present volume shows that the Poet was most at
home among his own lakes and mountains, and I
trust the division devoted to " The English Lake
District " (" Wordsworthshire," as it has not inaptly
been called) may be of real service to the Wordsworthian tourist among that " multitude of hills,
crags, woodlands, waterfalls, and rills."

The collection of " Familiar Quotations " is the
completest yet given ; and I have taken considerable
pains to include none but those used not unfrequently
in the pulpit, on the platform, and by the essayist.
By far the completest collection of " Familiar Quotations " from Wordsworth hitherto published is the
one included in Bartlett's *Familiar Quotations* (Boston
[U.S.A.], Little, Brown & Co., 1882). The present
volume contains about half as many more, and I
have been compelled to reject a few of those given
in the above-named work, for the reason that they
had not become sufficiently " familiar "—at any rate
in this country. I hope there may be *few* of those
given in my collection which are open to the
objection of unfamiliarity ; it has been carefully revised a number of times (and has passed through the
hands of several persons for that purpose), and a
number of passages have been finally rejected which
were originally inserted.

That Wordsworth, in the future, will be chiefly
read in Selection rather than in his entirety, it is safe
to predict. That very many thoughtful readers *now*
cannot tolerate him *as a whole* is a well-known fact.
For such the " List of Best Poems," in this volume,
may be of some service. In publishing this " List,"
I am, I am aware, challenging the verdict of several
editors of Wordsworth Anthologies. I have in-

cluded the names of a greater number of pieces than have ever been given in any of the published Selections—nearly twice as many as are given in the most popular one of all, Mr Matthew Arnold's. This I have done after mature reflection, and repeated examination of the whole of Wordsworth's poetry; and find that "the great and ample body of powerful work which remains to him, even after all his inferior work has been cleared away" (*Arnold*), is *much* greater than what is given in the great critic's "Selections." A careful examination of the Poet's whole work will, I venture to think, convince any discerning student that he has not got (in Mr Arnold's good selection) the whole of the "great and ample body of powerful work" which Wordsworth has left to us.

This volume more than fulfils the promise of its Prospectus. In it is included, as an Appendix, a hitherto unpublished cancelled version of the great "Ode to Duty," and Indices to all the Birds, Trees, Plants, and Flowers described by the Poet.

This Dictionary has been compiled from the text of the Poems as finally revised by Wordsworth. Those who consult the present work will have no difficulty in at once finding the passages or Poems they search for, if they possess a properly indexed edition of the works of the Poet. The following are the complete and authoritative editions of the Poet's works:—the later editions published by Moxon; those issued by Ward, Lock & Co. (in 6 vols.); Professor Knight's Library edition * (in 8 vols.); and the one-volume edition published by Macmillan & Co.

---

* It is much to be regretted that there has been no English edition of Wordsworth having the lines of the longer poems numbered, and that this otherwise admirable edition lacks this useful—and almost indispensable—feature of a Student's edition. In the case of *The Excursion* (Vol. V. of this edition) the numbers of the lines are given

In bringing this preface to a close I have to
acknowledge my indebtedness to Professor Knight
of St Andrews for his kind permission in respect of
his edition of Wordsworth's Poetical Works, his
"The English Lake District as Interpreted in the
Poems of Wordsworth," and his "Through the Wordsworth Country." These works have been of considerable service to me, especially in the preparation of the
topographical section of this book. But for the in-
formation these supplied my work would have been
imperfectly done. On everything that relates to the
topography of the poems of Wordsworth, Professor
Knight is the greatest authority.

In conclusion I have also to thank those gentle-
men who have rendered me good service in assisting
me in connection with the collection of "Familiar
Quotations." By means of their knowledge, this
portion of the volume has become, I feel sure, all the
more reliable.

                                    J. R. TUTIN.

HULL, 30*th April* 1891.

---

at the top of each page, but are incorrect throughout, the editor or
the compositor having counted the half lines at the beginning and end
of the paragraphs as, in each case, full ones. Consequently the line-
numbers, given in the following pages, do not correspond with the
incorrect numbering in this edition.

THE

WORDSWORTH DICTIONARY

OF

PERSONS.

I. Contemporary and Historical.

BACON (LORD), Philosopher. *School Exercise*, 1784.

BALBI. *Epitaphs from Chiabrera*, IX.

BARBAROSSA, EMPEROR, " Cæsar's Successor." *Ecclesiastical Sonnets*, Pt. I., xxxviii.

BAYARD (PIERRE), a celebrated French Warrior. *Descriptive Sketches.*

BEAUMONT (FRANCIS), Eng. Poet. *For a Seat in the Groves of Coleorton.*

BEAUMONT (SIR GEO. H.). *At Applethwaite, near Keswick.*

—————— *Elegiac Stanzas, suggested by a Picture of Peele Castle.*

—————— *Elegiac Stanzas* (" O for a dirge ").

—————— *Epistle to Sir G. H. Beaumont.*

— —————— *In the Grounds of Coleorton.*

—————— *Elegiac Musings in the Grounds of Coleorton Hall.*

—————— *In a Garden of the Same.*

—————— *Written at request of Sir G. H. Beaumont.*

—————— *For a Seat in the Groves of Coleorton.*

—————— *The Pine of Monte Mario at Rome.*

BEAUMONT (LADY). *To Lady Beaumont.*

BEAUPUIS (GENL.). *The Prelude*, Book IX., ll. 139-161.

—————— *The Prelude*, Book IX., ll. 419-430.

BECKET (THOS. À), Archbishop of Canterbury. *Ecclesiastical Sonnets*, Pt. I., xxxvii.

BEDE, "The Venerable," Historian. *Ecclesiastical Sonnets*, Pt. I., xxiii.

BELUS, King of Babylon. *Trans. of part of First Book of the Eneid.*

BEWICK (THOS.), Wood Engraver. *The Two Thieves.*

BITIAS, a Trojan, son of Alcanor. *Trans. of part of First Book of the Eneid.*

BOWES (SIR GEORGE). *The White Doe of Rylstone*, Canto VI.

BOYLE (ADMIRAL). *The Prelude*, Book VII., l. 166.

CAVENDISH [Duke of Devonshire]. *At Furness Abbey.*

CENI (FRANCESCO). *Epitaphs from Chiabrera,* I.

CERVANTES (Author of "Don Quixote"). *The Prelude,* Book V., ll. 61, 123.

CHARLES II., King of England. *The Excursion,* Book V., l. 187.

—————— *Ecclesiastical Sonnets,* Pt. III., iii.

CHATTERTON (THOS.), "the marvellous Boy." *Resolution and Independence,* VII.

CHAUCER (GEOFFREY), English Poet. *The Prelude,* Book III., ll. 275-278.

—————— *Liberty.*

CHIABRERA, Italian Poet. *Musings near Aquapendente.*

—————— *Epitaphs from Chiabrera,* V.

CHICHELY (ARCHBISHOP). *Ecclesiastical Sonnets,* Pt II., xv.

CLAPHAM (JOHN DE). *The White Doe of Rylstone,* Canto I.

CLARKSON (THOMAS). *To Thomas Clarkson.*

CLAUDE, daughter of Louis XII. *The Prelude,* Book IX., l. 484.

CLIFFORD (LORD), "the Shepherd." *Song at the Feast of Brougham Castle.*

—————— *The Borderers,* Acts I., III.

COLERIDGE (HARTLEY). *To H. C., Six Years Old.*

COLERIDGE (S. T.), "A noticeable man." *Written in Thomson's "Castle of Indolence."*

—————— *The Prelude,* Book II., ll. 451-471; Book III., ll. 317-321; Book VI., ll. 240-251; Book XIV., ll. 276-301; ll. 392-414.

—————— "Philosopher and Poet." *The Recluse,* Book I., l. 660.

—————— "The rapt one." *Effusion upon the Death of James Hogg.*

COLERIDGE (SARA), "Last of the Three." *The Triad.*

COLLINS (WM.), Eng. Poet. *Remembrance of Collins.*

COLUMBUS (CHRISTOPHER). *The Excursion,* Book VI., l. 234.

COMATES, "divine." *The Prelude,* Book XI., ll. 443-449.

COWLEY (ABRAHAM), English Poet, "the melancholy Cowley." *Liberty.*

CRABBE (GEO.), English Poet. *Effusion upon the Death of James Hogg.*

CRANMER (ARCHBISHOP), Martyr. *Ecclesiastical Sonnets,* Pt. II., xxxv.

CUTHBERT (ST) of Durham. *The White Doe of Rylstone,* Canto III.

DACRE (LORD). *The White Doe of Rylstone,* Canto III., IV.

DANTE ALIGHIERI, Italian Poet. "*Scorn not the Sonnet ; Critic, you have frowned.*"
—— *At Florence.*

DARLING (GRACE). *Grace Darling.*

DATI (ROBERTO). *Epitaphs from Chiabrera,* VI.

D'ENGHIEN, DUKE. *Feelings of a French Royalist.*

DIOCLETIAN, CAIUS VALERIUS, Roman Emperor. *Ecclesiastical Sonnets,* Pt. I., vi.

DION, Syracusan Statesman. *The Prelude,* Book IX., l. 409.

DION, disciple and friend of Plato. *Dion.*

DOMINIQUE DE GOURGUES, "that one Frenchman." *The Prelude,* Book I., ll. 206-212.

DOUGLAS, "degenerate." *Sonnet composed at —— Castle.*

DUDLEY (EARL). *The White Doe of Rylstone,* Canto III.

DUNDEE (VISCOUNT), a Scotch Royalist and Warrior. *Descriptive Sketches.*

DUNMAIL, KING, "last King of rocky Cumberland." *The Waggoner,* Canto I.

DYER (JOHN), Poet. *To the Poet, John Dyer.*

EDWARD. *School Exercise,* 1784.

EDWARD THE CONFESSOR. *Ecclesiastical Sonnets,* Pt. I., xxxi.

EDWARD III., King of England. *Ecclesiastical Sonnets,* Pt. II., vii.

EDWARD VI., King of England. *Ecclesiastical Sonnets,* Pt. II., xxxi., xxxii.

EDWIN, King of the Northumbrians. *Ecclesiastical Sonnets,* Pt. I., xv.

ELIZA [Queen Elizabeth]. *The Excursion,* Book VII., l. 925.

ELIZABETH (QUEEN). *Ecclesiastical Sonnets,* Pt. II., xxxviii.

EMMA [Dorothy Wordsworth]. *"There is a little unpretending Rill."*

EMPEDOCLES, a Sicilian Poet. *The Prelude,* Book XI., l. 434.

ERASMUS (DES.), a celebrated Dutch Author. *The Prelude,* Book III., ll. 474-478.

EUDEMUS, a Greek Philosopher. *The Prelude,* Book IX., l. 412.

FALKLAND (L. C., VISCOUNT). *Lines on the Expected Invasion,* 1803.

FENWICK (MISS). *On a Portrait of I. F., painted by Margaret Gillies.*
———— *To I. F. (" The star which comes").*

FERMOR (*Mrs*). *Elegiac Stanzas (" O for a dirge!").*
———— *Cenotaph.*

FISHER (JOHN), Bishop of Rochester. *Ecclesiastical Sonnets,* Pt. II., xxvi.

FITZGERALD (LADY). *To ——, in her seventieth year.*

FLAMINIUS, "vanquished chief." *Near the Lake of Thrasymene* (second Sonnet).

FLAMINIUS (T. QUINTIUS), "a Roman Master." *"A Roman Master stands on Grecian ground."*

FLEMING (REV. JOHN), the "Friend" in *The Prelude,* Book II., ll. 333-338.

98297

FLEMING (LADY). *To the Lady Fleming.*
FLETCHER (JOHN), Dramatist. *In the Grounds of Coleorton.*
FOX (CHAS. JAS.), Statesman. *Lines composed at Grasmere.*
FREDERICK THE WISE, Elector of Saxony. *Installation Ode*, 1847.

GEORGE III., King of England. *November*, 1813.
────── *On the Death of his Majesty.*
────── *Nov.*, 1813. ("*Now that all hearts are glad.*")
GESNER (SOLOMON), a German Poet, &c. *The Prelude*, Book VII., ll. 563-4.
GILLIES (MISS M.). *To a Painter.*
GILLIES (R. P.), Artist. "*From the dark chambers of dejection freed.*"
GIORDANO (LUCCA), Italian Painter. *To Lucca Giordano.*
GODDARD (FR. WM.). *Elegiac Stanzas* ("*Lulled by the sound*").
GORSAS, a French deputy. *The Prelude*, Book IX., l. 176.
GOUGH (CHARLES), the "Traveller" in *Fidelity.*
[GOUGH, JOHN], Botanist. *The Excursion*, Book VII., ll. 486-515.
GRAY (THOS.), English Poet. *The Prelude*, Book X., l. 536.
GREEN (GEORGE). *George and Sarah Green.*
GREEN (SARAH). *George and Sarah Green.*
GREENWOOD (ROBERT), "the Minstrel of the Troop." *The Prelude*, Book II., l. 168.
GUSTAVUS I., King of Sweden. *The Prelude*, Book I., ll. 211-212.
GUSTAVUS IV., "the royal Swede." "*Call not the royal Swede unfortunate.*"
────── *The King of Sweden.*

HARRINGTON (JAS.), Politician. "*Great men have been among us.*"

HAYDON (B. R.), Painter. *To B. R. Haydon.*

—— *To B. R. Haydon, on seeing his Picture of Napoleon Buonaparte.*

HEMANS (FELICIA D.), Poetess. *Effusion upon the Death of James Hogg.*

HENRY II., King of England. *Ecclesiastical Sonnets,* Pt. I., xxxvii.

HENRY V., King of England. *The Prelude,* Book VII., l. 498.

HENRY VI., King of England, "the royal Saint," *Ecclesiastical Sonnets,* Pt. III., xliii.

HENRY VIII., King of England. *The Excursion,* Book V., l. 182.

—— *Recollection of the Portrait of King Henry Eighth, Trinity Lodge, Cambridge.*

HERMODIUS, an Athenian. *The Prelude,* Book X., l. 198.

HOFFER (ANDREW), chief of the Tyrolese leaders. *Tyrolese Sonnets: I.—Hoffer.*

HOGG (JAMES), "the Ettrick Shepherd." *Effusion upon the Death of James Hogg.*

HOMER, "the great thunderer." *The Prelude,* Book V., l. 202.

HOMER, "Mæonides." *Written in a Blank leaf of Macpherson's Ossian.*

HOOKER (RICHARD), Divine. *Ecclesiastical Sonnets,* Pt. II., xxxix.

HORACE [=HORATIUS FLACCUS], the Latin Poet. *September,* 1819 (second Poem).

—— "the Sabine Bard." *The River Duddon,* I.

—— *Musings near Aquapendente.*

—— *Liberty.*

HOWARD (LORD WM.). *The White Doe of Rylstone,* Canto III., IV.

HOWARD (MRS). *Monument of Mrs Howard.*

HUTCHINSON (HENRY). *Isle of Man* ("*Did pangs of grief*").
—— *By a Retired Mariner.*
HUTCHINSON (JOANNA). *Naming of Places—To Joanna.*
HUTCHINSON (MARY). *To M. H.*
—— "*a gentle maid.*" *A Farewell.*
—— "*another maid.*" *The Prelude*, Book VI., ll. 224-236.
—— "*an inmate of the heart.*" *The Prelude*, Book XIV., ll. 266-275.
HUTCHINSON (SARA). *November*, 1836 ("*Even so for me a Vision sanctified*").
—— "*Forth from a jutting ridge around whose base.*"
—— *To S. H.*

JAMES II., "vacillating Bondman." *Ecclesiastical Sonnets*, Pt. III., ix.
JEWEL (BISHOP). *Ecclesiastical Sonnets*, Pt. II., xxxix.
JEWSBURY (ANNA). "*While Anna's peers and early playmates tread.*"
—— *Liberty.*
JOHN, King of England. *Ecclesiastical Sonnets*, Pt. I., xxxvii.
JONES (ROBERT). *Composed near Calais* ("*Jones! as from Calais*").
—— "*a youthful friend.*" *The Prelude*, Book VI., l. 323.
JONSON (BEN), Dramatist. *In the Grounds of Coleorton.*
JULIUS CÆSAR. *Artegal and Elidure.*
LAMB (CHARLES). *Written after the Death of Charles Lamb.*
—— *Effusion upon the Death of James Hogg.*
—— *Farewell Lines* ("'High bliss is only for a higher state'").

LATIMER (HUGH), Martyr. *Ecclesiastical Sonnets,* Pt. II., xxxiv.

LAUD (ARCHBISHOP). *Ecclesiastical Sonnets,* Pt. II., xlv.

LE BRUN (CHARLES), Painter. *The Prelude,* Book IX., ll. 77-80.

LEONIDAS [King of Sparta]. *Composed at Cora Linn.*

LEWTHWAITE (BARBARA). *The Pet-Lamb.*

LLOYD (REV. OWEN). *Epitaph in the Chapel-yard of Langdale, Westmoreland.*

LONSDALE (EARL). *The Excursion,* Dedicatory Sonnet.
——— *To the Earl of Lonsdale.*

LONSDALE (COUNTESS). *Lines written in the Album of the Countess of Lonsdale.*

LOWTHER (LADY MARY). *To the Lady Mary Lowther.*

LUTHER (MARTIN), Reformer. *Ecclesiastical Sonnets,* Pt. II., xxxvii.
——— *Installation Ode,* 1847.

MACKERETH (SARA), "the Westmoreland girl." *The Westmoreland Girl.*

MAHOMET, "Arabian Prophet." *Ecclesiastical Sonnets,* Pt. II., xxvii.

MARO [VIRGIL], the Roman Poet. *September,* 1819 (second Poem).

MARSHALL (CORDELIA). *To Cordelia M———, Hallsteads, Ullswater.*

MARVELL (ANDREW), Poet, &c. *"Great men have been among us."*

MARY, Queen of Scots. *Lament of Mary, Queen of Scots.*
——— *Captivity—Mary, Queen of Scots.*
——— *Mary, Queen of Scots* ("*Dear to the Loves*").

MELANCHTHON (P.), Reformer. *The Prelude,* Book III., ll. 474-478.

MILTON (JOHN), English Poet. *London,* 1802 ("*Milton, thou shouldst be living*").

NORTON (FRANCIS). *The White Doe of Rylstone,*
Canto II., III., IV., V., VI., VII.
NORTON (JOHN). *The White Doe of Rylstone,*
Canto II.
NORTON (MARMADUKE). *The White Doe of Rylstone,*
Canto II., VI.
NORTON (RICHARD). *The White Doe of Rylstone,*
Canto II.
NUMA [Numa Pompilius, second King of Rome]. *To
Lycoris* (second Poem).

ORPHEUS, a Thracian Musician and Poet. *Written
in a blank leaf of Macpherson's Ossian.*
OSSIAN, a Gaelic Bard. *Glen-Almain.*
—— *The Prelude,* Book VII., ll. 567-8.
—— *Effusion, in Pleasure Ground, Banks of Bran.*
—— *Written in a blank leaf of Macpherson's Ossian.*
—— *The Highland Broach.*

PALAFOX-Y-MELZI (DON J.), Governor of Saragossa.
"*And is it among rude untutored vales.*"
—— "*Ah! where is Palafox? nor tongue*"
PANDULPH, "a Proud Legate." *Ecclesiastical Sonnets,*
Pt. I., xxxvii.
PEMBROKE (EARL). *The White Doe of Rylstone,*
Canto I.
PENN (WILLIAM). *To the Pennsylvanians.*
PERCY, EARL OF NORTHUMBERLAND, 1377-1408.
Yew-trees.
PERCY (EARL). *The White Doe of Rylstone,* Canto
II., III.
PETRARCH, Italian Poet. "*Scorn not the Sonnet;
Critic, you have frowned.*"
PLATO, a celebrated Greek Philosopher. *The Prelude,*
Book IX., l. 409.
—— *Dion.*
—— *Epitaphs from Chiabrera,* IX.

PLINY, the Historian, author of "The Panegyric of Trajan." *The Pillar of Trajan.*

PONSONBY (HON. MISS). *To the Lady E. B. and the Hon. Miss P.*

POZZOBONNELLI (FRANCESCO). *Epitaphs from Chiabrera,* VIII.

PRIAM, King of Troy. *Trans. of part of First Book of The Eneid.*

QUILLINAN (JEMIMA). *Lines suggested by a Portrait.*
────── *In the Woods of Rydal.*

QUILLINAN (ROTHA), "my Spiritual Child." *To Rotha Q.*
────── the "bright Creature" of *To a Child. Written in her Album.*

RAPHAEL, Italian Painter. *A Jewish Family.*

REDING (ALOYS). *Memorial near the outlet of the Lake of Thun.*

REYNOLDS (SIR JOSHUA), Painter. *Written at the request of Sir George Beaumont.*

RICHARD I., King of England. *Ecclesiastical Sonnets,* Pt. I., xxxv.

RIDLEY (NICHOLAS), English Martyr. *Ecclesiastical Sonnets,* Pt. II., xxxiv.

ROBESPIERRE (MAXIMILIAN). *The Prelude,* Book X., ll. 101, 104, 500.

ROBIN HOOD, English Outlaw. *The Prelude,* Book V., l. 343.
────── *Rob Roy's Grave.*
────── *On the Detraction which followed the publication of a certain Poem.*
────── *The Triad.*

ROBINSON (HENRY CRABB). *To Henry Crabb Robinson.*

ROB ROY, a Scottish Outlaw. *Rob Roy's Grave.*
────── *On the Detraction which followed the publication of a certain Poem.*

ROLAND, MADAME [Jeanne-Marie Phlipon]. *The Prelude*, Book X., ll. 381-3.

ROLAND, a famous hero of France. *Aix-la-Chapelle.*

RUSSELL (LORD WM.), Patriot and Statesman. *Ecclesiastical Sonnets*, Pt. III., x.

SABRA, daughter of Ptolemy, King of Egypt. *The Prelude*, Book V., l. 344.

SACHEVEREL (HENRY), Divine. *Ecclesiastical Sonnets*, Pt. III., xi.

ST ALBAN, "England's first Martyr." *Ecclesiastical Sonnets*, Pt. I., vi.

ST ANNE. *The Excursion*, Book IV., l. 910.

ST AUGUSTINE, the Monk. *Ecclesiastical Sonnets*, Pt. I., xiv.

ST BARTHOLOMEW. *The Prelude*, Book VII., l. 678.

ST CATHERINE, of Ledbury. *St Catherine of Ledbury.*

ST COLUMBA, Irish Saint. *The Highland Broach.*

———— *"Homeward we turn. Isle of Columba's Cell."*

ST CUTHBERT. *For the Spot where the Hermitage stood on St Herbert's Island.*

———— *Grace Darling.*

ST DUNSTAN, an Anglo-Norman Ecclesiastic. *Ecclesiastical Sonnets*, Pt. I., xxviii.

ST FILLAN, a Scottish Saint. *The Excursion*, Book IV., l. 910.

ST FRANCIS OF ASSISI. *The Cuckoo at Laverna.*

ST GEORGE, National Saint of England. *The Prelude*, Book V., l. 344.

———— *Song at the Feast of Brougham Castle.*

———— "of England." *Protest against the Ballot.*

———— *Ecclesiastical Sonnets*, Pt. II., xxiv.

ST GILES [Patron Saint of Edinbro']. *The Excursion*, Book IV., l. 911.

ST MARGARET. *Ecclesiastical Sonnets*, Pt. II., xxiv.

SIMONIDES, "pure," a Greek Poet. *September,* 1819 (second Poem).

SOBIESKI (SIR JOHN), King of Poland. *Siege of Vienna raised by John Sobieski.*

SOUTHEY (EDITH), "Lucida" in *The Triad.*

S[OUTHEY], E. M. *On Seeing a Needlecase in the form of a Harp.*

SOUTHEY (MRS). "*Oh, what a Wreck! how changed in mien and speech.*"

SOUTHEY (ROBERT). *On Seeing a Needlecase in the form of a Harp.*

——— *Inscription for a Monument in Crosthwaite Church.*

SPENSER (EDMUND), English Poet. *The Prelude,* Book III., ll. 278-282; VI., l. 89.

——— *The Prelude,* Book VIII., l. 144.

——— "*Scorn not the Sonnet; Critic, you have frowned.*"

——— *Artegal and Elidure.*

SUSSEX (EARL). *The White Doe of Rylstone.* Canto V., VI.

TALIESIN, Bard and Cymric Chief. *Ecclesiastical Sonnets,* Pt. I., v., xii.

TASSO (TORQUATO). "*Scorn not the Sonnet; Critic, you have frowned.*"

——— *Musings near Aquapendente.*

TAYLOR (REV. WM.), "teacher of my youth." *The Prelude,* Book X., ll. 534-552.

——— *Matthew.*

——— *The Two April Mornings.*

——— *The Fountain.*

——— *Address to the Scholars of the Village School of* ——.

TELL (WILLIAM), Swiss Patriot and Hero. *Descriptive Sketches.*

——— *The Excursion,* Book VII., l. 810.

VERNON (MARY). " *By a blest Husband guided, Mary came.*"

VICTORIA, Queen. *Installation Ode,* 1847.

—— " *Deign, Sovereign Mistress, to accept a lay.*"

VIRGIL (" Maro "), the Roman Poet. *September,* 1819 (second Poem).

VIRIATUS, Lusitanian Chieftain. *Spanish Guerillas.*

VOLTAIRE, French Poet, &c. *The Excursion,* Book II., l. 42.

—— " The laughing Sage of France." *The Excursion,* Book IV., l. 996.

WALKER (SIR D.), " British Painter." *Lines Suggested by a Portrait.*

WALKER (MISS L.), " Lesbia." *To* —— (" *Wait, prithee, wait !* ").

WALKER (REV. ROBT.). *The River Duddon,* XVIII.

WALLACE (SIR WILLIAM), Scotch Patriot. *The Prelude,* Book I., ll. 214-220.

—— *The Triad.*

WALTON (ISAAC). *Written upon a blank leaf in* " *The Complete Angler.*"

—— *Ecclesiastical Sonnets,* Pt. III., v.

WELLINGTON (DUKE OF). *On a Portrait of the Duke of Wellington.*

WESTMORELAND (EARL). *The White Doe of Rylstone,* Canto III.

WHITE (DR), Bishop of Pennsylvania. *Ecclesiastical Sonnets,* Part III., xv.

WHITTINGTON (SIR R.). *The Excursion,* Book VII., ll. 91-92.

—— *The Prelude,* Book VII., ll. 112-115.

WICLIFFE (JOHN), English Reformer. *Ecclesiastical Sonnets,* Pt. II., xvii.

WILKINSON (THOMAS). *To the Spade of a Friend.*

WILLIAM III., King of England. *Ecclesiastical Sonnets,* Pt. III., ix.

WOLFE (GEN. JAMES). *Descriptive Sketches.*
WORDSWORTH (CATHERINE). *Characteristics of a Child three years old.*
WORDSWORTH (REV. DR C.). *To the Rev. Dr Wordsworth (with the Duddon Sonnets).*
——— *To the Rev. Christopher Wordsworth, D.D., Master of Harrow School.*
WORDSWORTH (DORA). *Address to my Infant Daughter Dora.*
——— "my little Dora." *The Kitten and the Falling Leaves.*
——— *The Longest Day.*
——— *The Contrast*, II.
——— "my own Dora." *"A little onward lend thy guiding hand."*
——— "youngest of the lovely Three." *The Triad.*
WORDSWORTH (DOROTHY), "my dear, dear Sister." *Tintern Abbey.*
——— "my Sister Emmeline." *The Sparrow's Nest.*
——— "my Sister Emmeline." *To a Butterfly.*
——— "my Lucy." *"Among all lovely things my love had been."*
——— "that sole sister." *The Prelude*, Book VI., ll. 198-203.
——— "the beloved sister." *The Prelude*, Book XI., ll. 335-354.
——— "a young enthusiast." *The Prelude*, Book XII., ll. 152-173.
——— "sister of my soul." *The Prelude*, Book XIV., ll. 232-266.
——— *The Recluse*, Book I., ll. 75-97.
——— "child of Nature." *To a Young Lady.*
——— *" There is a little unpretending rill."*
WORDSWORTH (JOHN), "my brother." *To the Daisy* (*"Sweet Flower!"*).
——— *Elegiac Stanzas, suggested by a Picture of Peel Castle.*

WORDSWORTH (JOHN), "my brother." *Elegiac Verses, in memory of my Brother, John Wordsworth.*

———— "a silent Poet," &c. "*When to the attractions of the busy world.*"

———— "Pilgrim of the Sea." *The Recluse,* Book I., l. 655.

WORDSWORTH (JOHN), the Poet's son. *To a Friend* ("Pastor and Patriot").

WORDSWORTH (MRS). "*She was a phantom of delight.*"

———— *On approaching Home* ("*Fly, some kind harbinger*").

———— *The White Doe of Rylstone. Dedication.*

———— *To* ——— ("*Let other bards*").

———— *To* ——— ("*O dearer far than light*").

———— *To a Painter.*

———— *On the same subject.*

———— "*Forth from a jutting ridge.*"

WORDSWORTH (THOS.), the Poet's son. "*Six months to six years added he remained.*"

WORDSWORTH (WM.), the Poet. *Expostulation and Reply.*

———— *The Tables Turned.*

———— *Written in Thomson's "Castle of Indolence."*

———— *In the Grounds of Coleorton.*

———— "*Adieu, Rydalian Laurels! that have grown.*"

———— *In Sight of the Town of Cockermouth.*

———— *Address from the Spirit of Cockermouth Castle.*

———— *Inscription intended for a Stone in the Grounds of Rydal Mount.*

———— *To the Author's Portrait.*

WORDSWORTH (W.), the Poet's son. *Isle of Man* ("*A youth too certain of his power*").

YOUNG, EDWARD (Author of "Night Thoughts"). *The Prelude,* Book VII., ll. 564-566.

II. MYTHICAL AND LEGENDARY.

ACHATES = A faithful friend. *Translation of part of First Book of the Eneid.*

ACHILLES, the Hero of Homer's Iliad. *Trans. of part of First Book of Eneid.*

ADAM BELL, a Northern Outlaw. *Suggested by a view from an Eminence in Inglewood Forest.*

ADONIS, a beautiful youth beloved of Venus. *Love lies bleeding.*

ÆNEAS, a Trojan prince, the hero of Virgil's epic. *Translation of part of The Eneid,* Book I.

ÆSON, son of Cretheus and Tyro. *Laodamia.*

AMPHITRITE, Queen of the Sea. *Fish Women.—On Landing at Calais.*

ANDATES [an ancient Goddess]. *The Excursion,* Book IX., l. 708.

ANGELICA, c. in Ariosto's "Orlando Furioso." *The Prelude,* Book IX., l. 451.

APOLLO, the God of Music. *The Excursion,* Book VII., l. 729.

——— "golden haired." *The Waggoner,* Canto IV.

——— *"I heard (Alas! 'twas only in a dream)."*

ARTEGAL, son of Gorlois, Prince of Cornwall. *Artegal and Elidure.*

ARTHUR (KING). *Artegal and Elidure.*

——— *The Egyptian Maid.*

ASCANIUS, son of Æneas. *Translation of part of The Eneid,* Book I:

ASTRAEA, the Goddess of Innocence. *The Italian Itinerant and Swiss Goatherd,* Pt. II.

AURORA, a goddess, daughter of Hyperion and Thea. *Trans. of part of First Book of The Eneid.*

BACCHUS, the God of Wine. *Ecclesiastical Sonnets,* Pt. II., xx.

BACCHUS, the God of Wine, *Trans. of part of First Book of the Eneid.*

BELLEROPHON, son of Glaucos. *" From the dark chambers of dejection freed."*

CHAM, "the Solar Deity." *Processions. Suggested on a Sabbath Morning in the Vale of Chamouny.*

CLIO, Muse of History. *Vernal Ode.*

———— *Plea for the Historian.*

CLYM O' THE CLOUGH, an noted outlaw. *Suggested by a view from an Eminence in Inglewood Forest.*

CORIN [= Corydon]. *The Prelude,* Book VIII., l. 285.

CORINEUS, a Trojan Chief. *Artegal and Elidure.*

CUPID, God of Love. *Translation of part of The Eneid,* Book I.

CYBELÈ, a goddess, wife of Saturn. *Processions. Suggested on a Sabbath Morning in the Vale of Chamouny.*

CYNTHIA [= the Moon]. *" Once I could hail (howe'er serene the sky)."*

———— *Echo, upon the Gemmi.*

———— *To Lucca Giordano.*

CYTHEREA [= Aphrodite], a Greek goddess. *Translation of part of The Eneid,* Book I.

DAPHNÈ, daughter of the God Peneus. *The Russian Fugitive,* Part III.

DIAN, "Goddess of the Chase." *Artegal and Elidure.*

DIAN, an ancient Goddess. *Ode to Lycoris,* I.

———— *The River Duddon,* XXII.

DIAN, the Goddess of Light. *" Once I could hail (howe'er serene the sky)."*

-———— *To the Lady Mary Lowther.*

———— *To Lucca Giordano.*

DIANA, Goddess of Hunting. *The Three Cottage Girls,* III.

DIANA, Goddess of Hunting. *The Excursion*, Book IV., ll. 865-871.

DIDO, Queen of Carthage. *Translation of part of The Eneid*, Book I.

DIOMED, King of Ætolia. *Trans. of part of First Book of The Eneid.*

ELIDURE, brother of Gorbonian, son of Morvidus. *Artegal and Elidure.*

ENDYMION. *To Lucca Giordano.*

ERMINIA, c. in Tasso's *Jerusalem Delivered*. *The Prelude*, Book IX.

EUPHROSYNE, one of the three Graces. *The Triad.*

FAIR ROSAMOND. *The Excursion*, Book VII., l. 90.

FINGAL, a Gaelic Hero. *Written in a blank leaf of Macpherson's Ossian.*

———— *Cave of Staffa* (three Sonnets).

———— *The Highland Broach.*

FLORIZEL, c. in Shakspere's "Winter's Tale." *The Prelude*, Book VIII., ll. 142-3.

FORTUNATUS. *The Prelude*, Book V., l. 342.

GANYMEDE [= Rosalind], c. in Shakspere's "As you like it." *The Prelude*, Book VIII., l. 141.

GANYMEDE, Jove's cup-bearer. *The Italian Itinerant and Swiss Goatherd*, Pt. I.

GORBONIAN, the son of Morvidus. *Artegal and Elidure.*

GUENDOLEN, daughter of Corineus, a Trojan Chief. *Artegal and Elidure.*

GUINEVER, c. in *Mort d'Arthur*. *The Egyptian Maid.*

HEBE, daughter of Jupiter. *School Exercise*, 1784.

HECTOR, son of Priam, King of Troy. *Laodamia.*

HECTOR, son of Priam, King of Troy. *Translation of part of First Book of The Eneid.*
HERCULES, son of Jupiter. *Laodamia.*
HERMES [Mercury], God of Speech. *Laodamia.*

IOPAS, King of Africa. *Translation of part of First Book of The Eneid.*
IRIS, the rainbow. *Ecclesiastical Sonnets*, Pt. II. xxii.
IULUS [= ASCANIUS], son of Æneas. *Translation of part of The Eneid*, Book I.
IZONDA, c. in *Mort d'Arthur.*   *The Egyptian Maid.*

JOVE, an ancient God. *"From the dark chambers of dejection freed."*
————— *Laodamia.*
————— *The Brownie's Cell*, St. X.
————— *Plea for the Historian.*
————— *" When haughty expectations prostrate lie."*
————— *Translation of part of First Book of The Eneid.*
JOVE, Ammonian. *Processions. Suggested on a Sabbath Morning in the Vale of Chamouny.*
JUNO, a beautiful Greek Goddess, and wife of Jupiter. *Translation of part of The Eneid, Book I.*
JUPITER. *Translation of part of First Book of The Eneid.*

LAODAMIA, wife of Protesilaus. *Laodamia.*
LEAR (KING), mythical King of Britain. *The Prelude*, Book X. l. 507.
————— *Artegal and Elidure.*
LYCORIS, the Cytheris of the poet Gallus. *Ode to Lycoris*, III.

MEDEA, daughter of Æetes, King of Colchis. *Laodamia.*
MERCURY, God of Speech and Eloquence. *Laodamia.*
MERLIN, Prince of Enchanters. *Artegal and Elidure.*

MERLIN, Prince of Enchanters. " *With how sad steps,
O Moon, thou climb'st the sky.*"
MERLIN, the Magician in *Mort d'Arthur. The
Egyptian Maid.*
MINERVA, the Goddess of Wisdom, War, &c. " *The
leaves that rustled on this oak-crowned hill.*"
MIRZA, a Persian Prince. " *The fairest, brightest hues
of ether fade.*"
MNEMOSYNE, " Sage." *Plea for the Historian.*

NEPTUNE, King of the Ocean. *Processions. Suggested
on a Sabbath Morning in the Vale of Chamouny.*
NINA, daughter of Tor-Thoma, a Scandinavian Chief.
The Egyptian Maid.

OBERON, " King of Faery." *The Triad.*
ODIN (= WODEN), a Scandinavian God. *The Pre-
lude,* Book I., ll. 169-170.
———— *At Rome. Regrets* (" Complacent Fictions ").

PAN, the God of Nature. *The Prelude,* Book VIII.,
ll. 183-5.
———— " *O'er the wide earth, on mountain and on
plain.*"
———— *Composed by the side of Grasmere Lake.*
———— " the shepherd's awe-inspiring God ! " *The
Excursion,* Book IV., ll. 886-887.
———— *The Excursion,* Book VII., l. 729.
———— *On the Power of Sound,* X.
PANDORUS, brother of Troilus. *Troilus and Cresida.*
PARCÆ, The Fates. *Laodamia.*
PHILOCTETES, arm-bearer of Hercules. " *When Philoc-
tetes in the Lemnian Isle.*"
PHYLLIS, the lover of Demophoon. *The Prelude,*
Book VIII. l. 287.

PROMETHEUS. *The Excursion*, Book VI. l. 539.

PROSERPINE, daughter of Ceres. "*Once I could hail (howe'er serene the sky)."*

PROTESILAUS, a famous Greek Warrior. *Laodamia.*

PROTEUS, the herdsman of Neptune. "*The World is too much with us."*

RHEA, an ancient Greek Goddess. *The Brownie's Cell*, St. X.

ROBIN GOOD-FELLOW (Puck), c. in "Midsummer Night's Dream." *The Whirlblast.*

ST CECILIA, the Patroness of Musicians. *Ecclesiastical Sonnets*, Pt. II., xxiv.
———— "*How rich that forehead's calm expanse!*"

SALII, Priests of Mars. *Processions. Suggested on a Sabbath Morning in the Vale of Chamouny.*

SATURN, a mythical King of Italy. *The Prelude*, Book VIII. l. 129.

SICHAEUS, a priest of Hercules' Temple. *Translation of part of First Book of The Eneid.*

SILENUS, a demi-god, attendant of Bacchus. *On the Power of Sound*, X.

SIR AGRAVAINE, c. in *Mort d'Arthur. The Egyptian Maid.*

SIR DINAS, c. in *Mort d'Arthur. The Egyptian Maid.*

SIR EGLAMORE, one of King Arthur's Knights. *The Somnambulist.*

SIR GALAHAD, c. in *Mort d'Arthur. The Egyptian Maid.*

SIR GAWAINE, c. in *Mort d'Arthur. The Egyptian Maid.*

SIR KAYE, c. in *Mort d'Arthur. The Egyptian Maid.*

SIR LAUNCELOT, c. in *Mort d'Arthur. The Egyptian Maid.*

SIR PERCIVAL, c. in *Mort d'Arthur*. *The Egyptian Maid.*

SIR TRISTRAM, c. in *Mort d'Arthur*. *The Egyptian Maid.*

TANTALUS, son of Jupiter. *The Excursion*, Book VI., l. 543.

TARANIS, a Gaelic God. *The Excursion*, Book IX., l. 704.

THOR, Scandinavian God of War, and son of Odin. *Ecclesiastical Sonnets*, Pt. I., xvii.

TRITON, son of Neptune. "*The World is too much with us.*"

UNA, c. in Spenser's "Faerie Queene." *An Evening Walk.*
——— *Personal Talk*, III.
——— *The White Doe of Rylstone. Dedication.*

URANIA, Muse of Astronomy. *The Recluse*, Book I. l. 778.
——— *Vernal Ode.*
——— *Written in a blank leaf of Macpherson's Ossian.*

VACUNA, a Sabine divinity. *Musings near Aquapendente.*

VENUS, Queen of Love. *Love lies bleeding.*
——— *Ecclesiastical Sonnets*, Pt. II., xx.
——— *The Birth of Love.*
——— *Trans. of part of First Book of The Eneid.*

WODEN (ODIN). *Ecclesiastical Sonnets*, Pt. I., xvii.
——— *The Prelude*, Book I., ll. 169-70.

YORDAS, "that Danish Witch." *The Prelude*, Book VIII., ll. 563-4.

III. BIBLICAL.

ADAM. *The Redbreast chasing the Butterfly.*

DANIEL, the Prophet. *The Two Thieves.*
———— *Picture of Daniel in the Lions' Den, at Hamilton Palace.*

ISAIAH. *The Prelude*, Book VII., l. 562.

JACOB, the Patriarch. *Humanity.*
JEHOVAH. *The Recluse*, Book I., l. 786.
JESUS. *Peter Bell : a Tale.*
———— *Inscriptions*, V. ("*Not seldom clad in Orient vest*").
———— *Ecclesiastical Sonnets*, I., viii. ; III., xiii.
———— *To the Lady Fleming* ("*When in the antique age*").
———— *Summer Tour*, 1833, XL. "*Tranquillity ! the sovereign aim.*"
JOB. *The Prelude*, Book VII., l. 562.
JOSEPH OF ARIMATHEA. *Ecclesiastical Sonnets*, Pt. II., xxi.
JOSHUA. *The Excursion*, Book VII., l. 813.

MARY, "Jesu's mother." *The Prioress' Tale, modernised.*
———— *Ecclesiastical Sonnets*, Pt. II., xxv.
———— *Our Lady of the Snow.*
———— *The Egyptian Maid.*
MOSES. *The Prelude*, Book VII., l. 563.

ST PAUL. *Ecclesiastical Sonnets*, Pt. I., ii.
ST JOHN. *The Brownie's Cell*, St. VI.
SAINT JOHN, "the Jewish Child." *A Jewish Family.*

SAINT JOHN. *The Prioress' Tale, modernised.*
ST JOHN, the Baptist. *Before the Picture of the Baptist, by Raphael.*
ST MAGDALENE. *Ecclesiastical Sonnets*, Pt. II., xxiv.
ST MICHAEL. *Ecclesiastical Sonnets*, Pt. II., xxiv.
ST PETER. *Ecclesiastical Sonnets*, Pt. I., ii.
SATAN. *To —— on her ascent of Helvellyn.*

IV. CHARACTERS OF FICTION.

ADAM, "old," of "Tilsbury Vale." *The Farmer of Tilsbury Vale.*
ADAM BRUCE. *Ellen Irwin.*
ALICE FELL. *Alice Fell.*
ALLAN. *Repentance, a Pastoral Ballad.*
ANCIENT MARINER, Coleridge's. *The Prelude*, Book XIV., l. 399.
ANDREW. *To a Sexton.*
——— *The Oak and the Broom.*
ANDREW JONES. *Andrew Jones.*
ANGELICA, c. in Tasso's *Jerusalem Delivered.* *The Prelude*, Book IX., l. 451.
ANNE. *Foresight.*

BARBARA. "*'Tis said that some have died for love.*"
BENJAMIN, "the Waggoner." *The Waggoner.*
BESS. *Peter Bell: a Tale.*
BETTY FOY. *The Idiot Boy.*

CATHERINE. *The Russian Fugitive*, Part III.
CHARLES FLEMING. *Rural Architecture.*
CHARLES. *Foresight.*
CHRISTABEL, Lady, c. in Coleridge's *Christabel.* *The Prelude*, Book XIV., ll. 400-1.
CRESIDA. *Troilus and Cresida.*
CRUSOE (ROBINSON). *To Enterprise.*

DESDEMONA, "the gentle lady."   *Personal   Talk,*
   III.

EDWARD.   *Anecdote for Fathers.*
———— *To my Sister.*
ELDRED, c. in *The Borderers.*
ELEANOR, c. in *The Borderers.*
ELLEN.   *The Excursion,* Book VI.
———— *The Childless Father.*
ELLEN IRWIN.   *Ellen Irwin.*
EMMA.   *Naming   of   Places* — " *It   was   an   April
   Morning.*"
———— *The Two April Mornings.*
———— *The Somnambulist.*
———— "*'Tis said that some have died for love.*"

FRANK.   *The Armenian Lady's Love.*

GEORGE FISHER.   *Rural Architecture.*
GERALDINE.   "*Ere with cold beads of midnight dew.*"
GIDEON.   *The Excursion,* Book VII., ll. 815-816.
GOODY BLAKE.   *Goody Blake and Harry Gill.*
GORDON.   *Ellen Irwin.*

HARRY GILL.   *Goody Blake and Harry Gill.*
HERBERT, c. in *The Borderers.*
HUBERT.   *The Horn of Egremont Castle.*

IDONEA, c. in *The Borderers.*

JAMES.   *The Idle Shepherd-Boys.*
JAMES EWBANK.   *The Brothers.*
JANE.   *We are Seven.*
———— *To a Sexton.*
JANE, wife of "Priest of Ennerdale."   *The Brothers.*
JOHN.   *We are Seven.*
JOHNNY.   *The Idiot Boy.*

JULIA. *The Prelude*, Book IX., l. 565.
——— c. in *Vaudracour and Julia.*
JULIET, c. in Shakspere's "Romeo and Juliet."
Vaudracour and Julia.

LACY, c. in *The Borderers.*
LENNOX, c. in *The Borderers.*
LEONARD. *The Brothers.*
LORD ARCHIBALD. *The Seven Sisters.*
LOUISA. *Louisa.*
LUCY. "*Strange fits of Passion.*"
——— "*She dwelt among the untrodden ways.*"
——— "*I travelled among unknown men.*"
——— "*Three years she grew in sun and shower.*"
——— "*A slumber did my spirit seal.*"
LUCY GRAY. *Lucy Gray.*
LUKE, son of Michael. *Michael.*

MABEL. *St Catherine of Ledbury.*
MARGARET. *The Excursion*, Book I.
MARMADUKE., c. in *The Borderers.*
MARTHA RAY. *The Thorn.*
MATTHEW. *Expostulation and Reply.*
——— "*Address to the Scholars of the Village School
of ——.*"
——— *Matthew.*
——— *The Two April Mornings.*
——— *The Fountain.*
MICHAEL. *Michael.*

OSWALD, c. in *The Borderers.*
——— *The Excursion*, Book VII., l. 756.

PERDITA, c. in Shakspere's "Winter's Tale." *The
Prelude*, Book VIII., ll. 142-3.
PETER BELL. *Peter Bell : A Tale.*
PETER BELL, referred to in *The Prelude*, Book XIV.,
ll. 404-6.

PHOEBE, c. in Shakspere's "As you like it." *The Prelude*, Book VIII., l. 141.

REGINALD SHORE. *Rural Architecture.*
RICHARD BATEMAN. *Michael.*
ROMEO, c. in Shakspere's "Romeo and Juliet." *Vaudracour and Julia.*
ROMILLY. *The Force of Prayer.*
RUTH. *Ruth.*

SIMON LEE. *Simon Lee.*
SIR ALFRED IRTHING. *The Excursion*, Book VII., l. 971.
SIR EUSTACE. *The Horn of Egremont Castle.*
SIR WALTER. *Hart-leap Well.*
SIR WILLIAM. *Written upon a Stone* ("*Stranger! this hillock*").
STEPHEN HILL. *The Thorn.*
STEPHEN OTTER. *Peter Bell: A Tale.*
SUSAN. *The Reverie of Poor Susan.*
———— *To a Sexton.*
SUSAN GALE. *The Idiot Boy.*

TAM O' SHANTER. *On the Detraction which followed the publication of a certain Poem.*
TIMOTHY. *The Childless Father.*
TROILUS. *Troilus and Cresida.*

VAUDRACOUR, c. in *Vaudracour and Julia.*
———— *The Prelude*, Book IX., l. 565.

WALLACE, c. in *The Borderers.*
WALTER. *The Idle Shepherd-Boys.*
WALTER EWBANK. *The Brothers.*
WILFRED. *The Thorn.*
———— c. in *The Borderers.*
WILFRED ARMATHWAITE. *The Excursion*, Book VI., l. 1079.

THE

WORDSWORTH DICTIONARY

OF

PLACES.

J. THE ENGLISH LAKE DISTRICT.*
(" WORDSWORTHSHIRE ").

" Dear native regions."
—*Extract from a Poem.*

" Among this multitude of hills,
Crags, woodlands, waterfalls, and rills."
—*The Waggoner.*

THE OUTLINES OF THE ENGLISH LAKE COUNTRY.

" I KNOW not how to give the reader a distinct image of these more readily, than by requesting him to place himself with me, in imagination, upon some given point; let it be the top of either of the mountains, Great Gavel, or Scawfel; or, rather, let us suppose our station to be a cloud hanging midway between those two mountains, at not more than half a mile's distance from the summit of each, and not many yards above their highest elevation; we shall then see stretched at our feet a number of vallies, not fewer than eight, diverging from the point, on which we are supposed to stand, like spokes from the nave of a wheel. First, we note, lying to the south-east, the vale of Langdale, which will conduct the eye to the long lake of Windermere, stretched nearly to the sea; or rather to the sands of the vast bay of Morcamb, serving here for the rim of this imaginary wheel; let us trace it in a direction from the south-east towards the south, and we shall next fix our eyes

---

* This is used in its wider significance as including the whole of the counties of Westmoreland and Cumberland, and that portion of North Lancashire known as the Furness District.

upon the vale of Coniston, running up likewise from
the sea, but not (as all the other vallies do) to the
nave of the wheel, and therefore it may be not inaptly
represented as a broken spoke sticking in the rim.
Looking forth again, with an inclination towards the
west, we see immediately at our feet the vale of
Duddon, in which is no lake, but a copious stream,
winding among fields, rocks, and mountains, and ter-
minating its course in the sands of Duddon. The
fourth vale, next to be observed, viz., that of the Esk,
is of the same general character as the last, yet beau-
tifully discriminated from it by peculiar features. Its
stream passes under the woody steep upon which
stands Muncaster Castle, the ancient seat of the
Penningtons, and after forming a short and narrow
æstuary enters the sea below the small town of Raven-
glass. Next, almost due west, look down into, and
along the deep valley of Wastdale, with its little
chapel, and half a dozen neat dwellings scattered
upon a plain of meadow and corn-ground intersected
with stone walls apparently innumerable, like a large
piece of lawless patch-work, or an array of mathemati-
cal figures, such as in the ancient schools of geometry
might have been sportively and fantastically traced
out upon sand. Beyond this little fertile plain lies,
within a bed of steep mountains, the long, narrow,
stern, and desolate lake of Wastdale; and, beyond
this, a dusky tract of level ground conducts the eye
to the Irish Sea. The stream that issues from Wast-
water is named the Irt, and falls into the æstuary of
the river Esk. Next comes in view Ennerdale, with
its lake of bold and somewhat savage shores. Its
stream, the Ehen or Enna, flowing through a soft and
fertile country, passes the town of Egremont, and the
ruins of the castle,—then, seeming, like the other
rivers, to break through the barrier of sand thrown up
by the winds on this tempestuous coast, enters the

Irish Sea. The vale of Buttermere, with the lake and village of that name, and Crummock - water, beyond, next present themselves. We will follow the main stream, the Coker, through the fertile and beautiful vale of Lorton, till it is lost in the Derwent, below the noble ruins of Cockermouth Castle. Lastly, Borrowdale, of which the vale of Keswick is only a continuation, stretching due north, brings us to a point nearly opposite to the vale of Winandermere with which we began. From this it will appear, that the image of a wheel, thus far exact, is little more than one half complete ; but the deficiency on the eastern side may be supplied by the vales of Wytheburn, Ulswater, Hawswater, and the vale of Grasmere and Rydal; none of these, however, run up to the central point between Great Gavel and Scawfell. From this, hitherto our central point, take a flight of not more than four or five miles eastward to the ridge of Helvellyn, and you will look down upon Wytheburn and St John's Vale, which are a branch of the vale of Keswick ; upon Ulswater, stretching due east :—and not far beyond to the south-east (though from this point not visible), lie the vale and lake of Hawswater ; and lastly, the vale of Grasmere, Rydal, and Ambleside, brings you back to Winandermere, thus completing, though on the eastern side in a somewhat irregular manner, the representative figure of the wheel."—*Guide to the Lakes : Description of the Scenery*, Section first.

AIRA-FORCE. *Summer Tour*, 1833, XLVI. — *The Somnambulist*.

AIREY-FORCE VALLEY. *Airey-force Valley*.

AMBLESIDE. " *While beams of orient light shoot wide.*"

APPLEBY CASTLE. *Feast of Brougham Castle*.

APPLETHWAITE, near Keswick. *At Applethwaite, near Keswick*.

ARMBOTH ("Armath")   *Verse Fragments.*

BEKANGS GHYLL, Low Furness.   *To the Lady Fleming,* II.

BIRKS BRIG, Duddon Valley.   *The River Duddon,* XI.

BLACK COMB.   *Epistle to Sir G. H. Beaumont.*
———— *Written on a Stone on the Side of Black Comb.*
———— *View from the Top of Black Comb.*
———— *Summer Tour,* 1833, XII.—*In the Channel.*

BLEA TARN VALLEY, Little Langdale.   *The Excursion,* Book II., ll. 327-687; III., ll. 1-100; IV.; V., ll. 1-16.

BLEA TARN COTTAGE, Little Langdale.   *The Excursion,* Book II. ll. 153-4, 338-342, 636-687; V. l. 1; IX., l. 774.

BLEA TARN.   *The Excursion,* Book II., l. 337; IV., l. 457.

BLENCATHARA.   *The Waggoner,* Canto IV.

BLENCATHARA [=Saddleback].   *Feast of Brougham Castle.*

BOOTLE.   *Epistle to Sir G. H. Beaumont.*

BORDER BEACON, near Penrith.   *The Prelude,* Book VI., l. 233.

BORROWDALE.   *Yew Trees.*

BOWNESS.   *The Prelude,* Book II., ll. 139-160.

BOWSCALE-TARN.   *Feast of Brougham Castle.*

BRIGHAM, NUN'S WELL.   *Summer Tour,* 1833, VIII.
—*Nun's Well, Brigham.*

BROTHERS WATER, Paterdale.   *Written in March.*
———— *Verse Fragments.*

B R O U G H [Brough-under-Stainmore].   *Feast of Brougham Castle.*

BROUGHAM CASTLE.   *The Prelude,* Book VI., ll. 205-206.
———— *Song at the Feast of Brougham Castle.*

DERWENT, RIVER.   *Summer Tour,* 1833, V.—*To the River Derwent.*
———— *Summer Tour,* 1833, VIII.—*Nun's Well.*
———— *Summer Tour,* 1833, IX.—*To a Friend.*
DERWENTWATER, FLOATING ISLAND.   *Floating Island.*
DERWENT-WATER, ST HERBERT'S ISLAND.   *Where the Hermitage stood on St Herbert's Island.*
DONNERDALE.   *The River Duddon,* XIII., XX.
DUDDON, RIVER.   *The River Duddon.*   (Sonnets.)
———— *Ecclesiastical Sonnets,* Part I., i.
DUDDON SANDS.   *The River Duddon,* XXXII.
DUDDON VALLEY.   *The Excursion,* Book VII., l. 315.
DUNGEON-GHYLL FORCE, G. Langdale.   *The Idle Shepherd-Boys.*
DUNMAIL RAISE.   *The Excursion,* Book VII., ll. 47-49.
———— *The Waggoner,* Canto I.
———— *Michael.*

EASEDALE.   *Michael.*
EASEDALE BECK.   " *It was an April Morning.*"
EDEN, RIVER.   *Summer Tour,* 1833, XXXVIII.—*The River Eden.*
———— *Long Meg and her Daughters.*
EGREMONT.   *The Brothers.*
EGREMONT CASTLE.   *The Horn of Egremont Castle.*
EMONT, RIVER.   *The Prelude,* Book VI., l. 204.
———— *Feast of Brougham Castle.*
———— *To the Spade of a Friend.*
ENNA, RIVER.   *The Brothers.*
ENNERDALE.   *The Brothers.*
ENNERDALE, PILLAR ROCK.   *The Brothers.*
ESTHWAITE VALE.   *Lines left upon a Seat in a Yew Tree.*
———— *The Prelude,* Book I., ll. 304-325 ; II., ll. 193-197 ; IV., l. 19 ; V., ll. 390-394 ; VI., l. 1.

GRASMERE. *Tour on Continent,* 1820, XXVI.—*The Eclipse of the Sun.*

GRASMERE CHURCH. *The Excursion,* Book VII., ll. 974-5 ; IX., ll. 575-579, 725.

———— *The Westmoreland Girl,* Part II.

———— (interior). *The Excursion,* Book V., ll. 138-217.

GRASMERE CHURCHYARD. *The Excursion,* Book V., l. 134 ; VI., ll. 605-610 ; VII., ll. 31-37.

GRASMERE, DOVE COTTAGE. *A Farewell.*

———— *Admonition.*

———— *Personal Talk,* I.

———— *The Prelude,* Book I., l. 74.

———— *The Recluse,* l. 300.

———— *The Waggoner,* Canto I.

GRASMERE, DOVE COTTAGE ORCHARD. *The Green Linnet.*

———— *To a Butterfly.*

———— *The Redbreast chasing the Butterfly.*

———— *The Kitten and the Falling Leaves.*

GRASMERE, DOVE COTTAGE GARDEN. *The Kitten and the Falling Leaves.*

GRASMERE, FIR GROVE. *The Recluse,* ll. 384-399.

GRASMERE, GREEN-HEAD GHYLL. *Michael.*

GRASMERE, JOHN'S GROVE, near the Wishing Gate. *The Prelude,* Book VII., ll. 44-47.

GRASMERE LAKE. *The Recluse,* l. 118.

———— *Composed by the side of Grasmere Lake.*

———— "*The leaves that rustled on this oak-crowned hill.*"

———— *Verse Fragments : To the Evening Star.*

GRASMERE LAKE, ISLAND ON. *An Evening Walk.*

———— *The Recluse,* l. 119.

———— *Written upon a Stone on the Island at Grasmere.*

GRASMERE, LANCRIGG TERRACE. "*Mark the con-centred hazels.*"

HAWKSHEAD.   *The Excursion*, Book I., l. 52 ; VI., l. 407.

HAWKSHEAD BECK.   *The Fountain.*

HAWKSHEAD CHURCH.   *The Prelude*, Book IV., ll. 21-23 ; V., ll. 392-403.

HAWKSHEAD CHURCHYARD.   " *There was a boy.*"

HAWKSHEAD SCHOOL.   *The Prelude*, Book V., ll. 393, 405.

—— *Address to Scholars of the Village School of ——.*

—— *Matthew.*

HELM CRAG, Grasmere.   *To Joanna.*

—— *The Waggoner*, Canto I.

HELVELLYN.   *To Joanna.*

—— *The Prelude*, Book VI., l. 208; VIII., ll. 1-4.

—— *The Recluse*, l. 518.

—— *Fidelity.*

—— *The Waggoner*, Canto II.

—— *To ——, on her ascent of Helvellyn.*

—— *Tour on Continent*, 1820, XXVI.—*The Eclipse of the Sun.*

—— *Summer Tour*, 1833, XLVII.—*To Cordelia M——.*

—— *Tour in Italy*, 1837, I.—*Musings near Aquapendente.*

—— *Verse Fragments.*

HIGH RIGG (" Nathdale Fell ").   *The Waggoner*, Canto IV.

HILLBECK, the " little humble stream."   *Song at the Feast of Brougham Castle.*

IRONKELD.   *The Prelude*, Book I., l. 370.

KIRKSTONE.   *To Joanna.*

KIRKSTONE, PASS OF.   *The Pass of Kirkstone.*

LANGDALE CHAPEL, Chapel Stile.   *Epitaph in the Chapel-Yard of Langdale.*

LANGDALE, GREAT. *The Idle Shepherd-Boys.*
——— *The Excursion*, Book II., ll. 90-104, 317.
LANGDALE, LITTLE. *The Excursion*, Book V., ll. 66-76.
LANGDALE PIKES. *The Excursion*, Book II., ll. 691-725.
——— *November* 1. (*"How clear"*)
LEGBERTHWAITE DALE. *Rural Architecture.*
LINGMOOR. *The Excursion*, Book II., ll. 323.
LODORE WATERFALL. *An Evening Walk.*
——— *The Spot where the Hermitage stood on St Herbert's Island.*
LORTON VALE. *Yew Trees.*
LOUGHRIGG. *To Joanna.*
——— *The Excursion*, Book IX., l. 570.
——— *"Aerial Rock—whose solitary brow."*
LOUGHRIGG FELL. *The Excursion*, Book IX., l. 609.
——— *"I watch, and long have watched."*
LOUGHRIGG TARN. *Epistle to Sir G. H. Beaumont.*
LOWTHER CASTLE. *Summer Tour*, 1833, XLIV.—*Lowther.*
LOWTHER, RIVER. *To Earl of Lonsdale.*
——— *Lines written in Album of Countess Lonsdale.*
LYULPH'S TOWER, Ulswater. *Summer Tour*, 1833, XLVI.—*The Somnambulist.*

MORECAMBE BAY. *The Excursion*, Book VII., l. 603.
MORESBY. *On a High Part of the Coast of Cumberland.*
——— *Composed by the Sea-Shore.*
MOSEDALE (north of Saddleback). *Feast of Brougham Castle.*

NATHDALE FELL (High Rigg). *The Waggoner.* Canto IV.
NUNNERY. *Summer Tour*, 1833, XLI.—*Nunnery.*

ORREST-HEAD, Windermere. *On the projected Kendal and Windermere Railway.*

PATERDALE. *The Excursion*, Book II., ll. 827-880.
PENDRAGON CASTLE. *Feast of Brougham Castle.*
PENRITH, COUNTESS' PILLAR, near. *Countess' Pillar.*
PENRITH, ROMAN STATION. *Roman Antiquities.*

RAVEN-CRAG. *The Waggoner*, Canto IV.
RED TARN, Helvellyn. *Fidelity.*
ROTHA, RIVER. *To Joanna.*
———— *The Prelude*, Book IX., l. 392.
———— *To Rotha Q——.*
RYDAL. *Composed at Rydal, on May Morning.*
RYDAL CHAPEL. *To the Lady Fleming.*
———— *On the same occasion.*
RYDAL COVE. *To the Lady Fleming*, IX.
RYDAL LAKE. *The Excursion*, Book IX., ll. 420-451.
———— *The Waggoner*, Canto I.
———— *September* 1819.
———— *" Soft as a cloud is yon blue Ridge."*
———— *By the Side of Rydal Mere.*
RYDAL LAKE, ISLAND ON. *The Wild Duck's Nest.*
———— *Written upon a Stone on one of the Islands at Rydal.*
RYDAL MOUNT. *The Longest Day.*
———— *The Cuckoo-Clock.*
———— *The Redbreast.*
———— *Ode to Lycoris.*
———— *Lament of Mary, Queen of Scots.*
———— *The Contrast*, II.
———— *" The Massy Ways, carried across these heights."*
———— *" This lawn, a carpet all alive."*
———— *Summer Tour*, 1833, I.
———— *Inscriptions* ("*In these fair vales*").
RYDAL MOUNT, "ELFIN POOL" IN "DORA'S FIELD." *Liberty.*

SKIDDAW.   *At the Grave of Burns.*
———— *The Prelude*, Book I., l. 295.
———— *The Waggoner*, Canto IV.
———— *Inscription* ("*Ye vales and hills*").
STICKLE TARN.   *The Excursion*, Book IV., ll. 402-412, and 1156-1187.
STONE ARTHUR.   "*There is an Eminence,—of these our hills.*"
STRIDING-EDGE, Helvellyn.   *Verse Fragments.*

TARN BECK, Duddon Valley.   *The River Duddon*, XIX.
THIRLMERE.   *Verse Fragments.*
———— "CHERRY TREE" INN.   *The Waggoner*, Canto II.
THIRLMERE, ROCK OF NAMES.   *The Waggoner*, Notes.
THRELKELD HALL.   *The Waggoner*, Canto IV.
THURSTON-MERE [Coniston Water].   *The Prelude*, Book VIII., l. 459.

ULLSWATER.   "*I wandered lonely as a cloud.*"
ULPHA CHURCH, Duddon Valley.   *The River Duddon*, XXXI.

WANSFELL.   "*Wansfell! this Household has a favored lot.*"
WATERHEAD ("the lowly Grange"), Coniston.   *Epistle to Sir G. H. Beaumont.*
WESTMORELAND.   *The Prelude*, Book VIII., ll. 428-429.
WETHERLAM.   *The Prelude*, Book I., ll. 378-400.
———— (?) *The Prelude*, Book II., l. 185.
WINDERMERE, LAKE.   *An Evening Walk.*
———— "*There was a Boy; ye knew him well, ye cliffs.*"
———— *The Prelude*, Book II., ll. 55-65 ; IV. ll. 5-17.
———— *The Waggoner*, Canto III.

WINDERMERE, LAKE. *The Excursion*, Book IX., l. 584.
—— *Tour on Continent*, 1820, XXVI.—*The Eclipse of the Sun.*
WINDERMERE, BROOK near LOWWOOD. *" There is a little unpretending Rill."*
WINDERMERE LAKE, ISLANDS ON. *The Prelude*, Book II., ll. 59-65 ; V., l. 365.
WORKINGTON, Cumberland. *Summer Tour*, 1833, X.—*Mary Queen of Scots.*
WRAY GHYLL FORCE. *The Excursion*, Book VI., l. 524-526.
WRYNOSE FELL. *The River Duddon*, I., II., III.
WYTHEBURN CHAPEL. *The Waggoner*, Canto II.
—— *The Excursion*, Book VII., ll. 140-144.

YEWDALE. *The Prelude*, Book I., ll. 326-339.
—— *Epistle to Sir G. H. Beaumont.*

II. OTHER PARTS OF ENGLAND.

" The sea surrounds
This favoured Land. . . .
. . . Swelling hills, and spacious plains
Besprent from shore to shore with steeple-towers."
—*The Excursion*, Book VI.

AMERDALE [= Littondale]. *The White Doe of Rylstone*, Canto IV.
AVON, RIVER (Lower), trib. of Severn. *Ecclesiastical Sonnets*, Pt. II., 17.

BARDEN, Craven, Yorkshire. *The White Doe of Rylstone*, Canto I.
BARDEN WOODS, Craven, Yorkshire. *The Force of Prayer.*

BARNARD CASTLE, Durham. *The White Doe of Rylstone,* Canto IV.

BISHOPSTONE, ANTIQS. AT, Herefordshire. *Roman Antiquities discovered at Bishopstone.*

BOLTON PRIORY, Yorkshire. *The White Doe of Rylstone,* Cantos I., V., VI. VII.
——— *The Force of Prayer.*

BOSWORTH FIELD, Leicestershire. *Feast of Brougham Castle.*

BRANCEPETH CASTLE, Durham. *The White Doe of Rylstone,* Canto III.

BUXTON, Derbyshire. *The Excursion,* Book VIII., l. 377.

CAERLEON, Monmouthshire. *The Egyptian Maid.*

CAMBRIDGE. *The Prelude,* Book VI.
——— *Installation Ode,* 1847.
——— *Ecclesiastical Sonnets,* Pt. III., 42.

CAMBRIDGE, HOOP INN. *The Prelude,* Book III., l. 17.

CAMBRIDGE, KING'S COLLEGE CHAPEL. *The Prelude,* Book III., ll. 4-6.
——— *Ecclesiastical Sonnets,* Pt. III., 43-45.

CAMBRIDGE, MAGDALENE BRIDGE. *The Prelude,* Book III., l. 16.

CAMBRIDGE, ST JOHN'S COLLEGE. *The Prelude,* Book III., ll. 46-63.

CAMBRIDGE, TRIN. COLL., NEWTON'S STATUE IN ANTE-CHAPEL OF. *The Prelude,* Book III., ll. 60-63.

CAM, RIVER, Cambridgeshire. *The Prelude,* Book III., l. 16 ; VI., l. 308.
——— *Oxford, May* 30, 1820.
——— *Ecclesiastical Sonnets,* Pt. III., 42.
——— *Liberty.*
——— *Installation Ode,* 1847.

CARLISLE. *Peter Bell,* Pt. I.

FOTHERINGAY, Northamptonshire. *Summer Tour, 1833*, X.—*Mary Queen of Scots.*

GLASTONBURY, Somersetshire. *Ecclesiastical Sonnets, Part II., 21.*

GORDALE SCAR, near Malham, W. Yorks. *Gordale.*

HAMBLETON HILLS, Yorkshire. *Composed after a journey across the Hambleton Hills.*

HARROW HILL, Middlesex. *To Rev. C. Wordsworth, D.D., Master of Harrow School.*

HART-LEAP WELL, near Richmond, Yorks. *Hart-leap Well.*

HAWES, Yorkshire. *Hart-leap Well.*

HULL, E. Yorkshire. *The Sailor's Mother* (ed. 1807).

KILVE, Somersetshire. *Anecdote for Fathers.*

KNARESBOROUGH, ST ROBERT'S CHAPEL, Yorkshire. *Effusion, Banks of the Bran.*

LANCASTER CASTLE. *Sonnets, Punishment of Death,* I.

LANCASTER, WEEPING HILL. *Sonnets, Punishment of Death,* I.

LEDBURY, Herefordshire. *St Catherine of Ledbury.*

LEEDS, Yorkshire. *Peter Bell,* Part I.

LEE, RIVER, Middlesex. *Written in "The Complete Angler."*

LEMING [LEEMING] LANE, Yorkshire. *Peter Bell,* Part III.

LINCOLN. *Peter Bell,* Part I.

LINCOLN CATHEDRAL. *Ecclesiastical Sonnets,* Part III., 42.

LISWYN, Monmouthshire (?). *Anecdote for Fathers.*

LITTONDALE ("Amerdale"). *The White Doe of Rylstone,* Canto VII.

LONDON. *Written in London, September* 1802.

MALVERN, Worcestershire. *St Catherine of Ledbury.*

NIDD, RIVER, Yorkshire. *Effusion, Banks of Bran.*
NORTON TOWER, Craven, Yorkshire. *The White Doe of Rylstone*, Canto V.

OKER HILL, Darley Dale, Derbyshire. *A Tradition of Oker Hill.*
OTTER, RIVER, Devonshire. *The Prelude*, Book VI., l. 272.
OXFORD. *Oxford, May* 30, 1820.
OXFORD CATHEDRAL. *Ecclesiastical Sonnets*, Pt. III., xlii.

PENDLE-HILL, Lancashire. *The White Doe of Rylstone*, Canto V.
PENNYGENT, mountain in Yorkshire. *The White Doe of Rylstone*, Canto V.

QUANTOCK, Somersetshire. *Ruth.*
QUANTOCK HILLS, Somersetshire. *The Thorn.*
—— *The Prelude*, Book XIV., ll. 396-397.

RABY HALL, Yorkshire. *The White Doe of Rylstone*, Canto III.
RICHMOND, Surrey. *Remembrance of Collins.*
—— *June*, 1820.
RICHMOND, Yorkshire. *Hart-leap Well.*
RYLSTONE BECK, Wharfedale, Yorkshire. *The White Doe of Rylstone*, Canto VII.
RYLSTONE FELL, Yorkshire. *The White Doe of Rylstone*, Canto V.
RYLSTONE HALL, Yorkshire. *The White Doe of Rylstone*, Canto II., IV., V., VI., VII.

SALISBURY PLAIN, Wiltshire. *Guilt and Sorrow.*
—— *The Prelude*, Book XIII., ll. 313-349.
—— *Ecclesiastical Sonnets*, Pt. I., v.
SARUM, Wiltshire. *Peter Bell*, Pt. I.

SEDBERGH, Yorkshire. *The Recluse*, l. 157.

SHAWFORD BROOK (River Sow), Staffordshire. *Written in " The Complete Angler."*

SKIPTON, Yorkshire. *Song at the Feast of Brougham Castle.*

SOCKBURN-ON-TEES, Durham. *The Prelude*, Book I., l. 62.

SOW, RIVER, near Eccleshall, Staffordshire ("Shawford Brook "). *Written in " The Complete Angler."*

STONE-HENGE, Salisbury Plain, Wiltshire. *Guilt and Sorrow*, XIV.

—— *The Excursion*, Book III., ll. 143-148.

STRID, THE (River Wharfe), West Yorkshire. *The Force of Prayer.*

SWALE, RIVER, Yorkshire. *Peter Bell*, Pt. I.

—— *Hart-leap Well.*

—— *The White Doe of Rylstone*, Canto III.

TEES, RIVER. *The White Doe of Rylstone*, Canto III., IV.

THAMES, RIVER. *Remembrance of Collins.*

—— *Lines written while sailing in a boat.*

—— *The Prelude*, Book VII., l. 129.

—— *Stray Pleasures.*

—— *The River Duddon : Dedication.*

—— *The River Duddon*, XXXII.

—— *Oxford, May* 30, 1820.

—— *June* 1820.

—— *Ecclesiastical Sonnets*, Pt. I., xxxi.

—— *Ecclesiastical Sonnets*, Pt. III., viii.

TINTERN ABBEY, Monmouthshire. *Lines composed a few miles above Tintern Abbey.*

TONE, RIVER, Somersetshire. *Ruth.*

TROMPINGTON, near Cambridge. *The Prelude*, Book III., l. 275.

TROYNOVANT, Trinovantum [= London]. *Artegal and Elidure.*

TWEED, RIVER, Berwickshire. *The Borderers*, Act I.
TYNE, RIVER, Northumberland. *The Two Thieves.*
———— *The White Doe of Rylstone*, Canto III.
———— *Ecclesiastical Sonnets*, Pt. I., xxxi.

URE (OR YORE), RIVER, Yorkshire. *Hart-leap Well.*
———— *The White Doe of Rylstone*, Canto III.

WALTHAM ABBEY, Essex. *Ecclesiastical Sonnets*,
Pt. II., xxi.
WENSLEYDALE, Yorkshire. *The Recluse*, l. 157.
WENSLEY MOOR, Yorkshire. *Hart-leap Well.*
WERE, RIVER, Durham. *The White Doe of Rylstone*,
Canto III.
WETHERBY, Yorkshire. *The White Doe of Rylstone*,
Canto III.
WHARFE, RIVER, Yorkshire. *The White Doe of
Rylstone*, Canto I., VII.
———— *The Force of Prayer.*
WINDSOR, Berkshire. *Ecclesiastical Sonnets*, Pt. II., vi.
WORCESTER CATHEDRAL. *A Gravestone in the
Cloisters of Worcester Cathedral.*
WYE, RIVER, Monmouthshire. *Lines composed a few
miles above Tintern Abbey.*

YORK. *Peter Bell*, Part I.
———— *The White Doe of Rylstone*, Canto V.
YORK CATHEDRAL. *Ecclesiastical Sonnets*, Pt. III.,
xlii.

III. WALES.

*" Through the . . . tracts
Of Cambria ranging."*
—*The Prelude*, Book XIV

BANGOR. *Ecclesiastical Sonnets*, Pt. I., xii.
BETHGELERT, N. Wales. *The Prelude*, Book XIV.,
l. 4.

CADER IDRIS. *The Excursion,* Book VII., 1. 8.
CAERNARVON. *Peter Bell,* Pt. I.
CARNARVON CASTLE, N. Wales. *Composed among the Ruins of a Castle in N. Wales.*
CARDIFF, S. Wales. *" When Severn's sweeping flood."*
CONWAY, N. Wales. *We are Seven.*

DEE, RIVER, N. Wales. *To the Lady E. B. and the Hon. Miss P.*
DEVIL'S BRIDGE, Hafod (Wales). *To the Torrent at the Devil's Bridge.*

GLYN MYRVR, N. Wales. *To the Lady E. B. and the Hon Miss P.*
GRONGAR HILL, S. Wales. *To the Poet, John Dyer.*

IVOR-HALL, Cardiganshire. *Simon Lee.*

MENAIS STRAIT, Anglesea. *Ecclesiastical Sonnets,* Part I., iii.

PENMANMAUR. *The Excursion,* Book VII., 1. 8.
PLASS NEWIDD, N. Wales. *To the Lady E. B. and the Hon. Miss P.*
PLINLIMMON, N. Wales. *Ecclesiastical Sonnets,* Part I., x.

SEVERN, RIVER, Montgomeryshire. *Ecclesiastical Sonnets,* Part II., xvii.
SEVERN, RIVER. *" When Severn's sweeping flood."*
SNOWDON, mountain in N. Wales. *The Prelude,* Book XIV., ll. 6-62.
—— *The Excursion,* Book VII., l. 7.
—— *To the Poet, John Dyer.*
—— *Ecclesiastical Sonnets,* Pt. I., v.

IV. Isle of Man.

" Mona's miniature."
—*Summer Tour*, 1833, XXI.

BALA-SALA. *Summer Tour*, 1833. XX.—*At Bala-Sala.*

DOUGLAS, TOWER OF REFUGE. *Summer Tour*, 1833, XII.—*On entering Douglas Bay.*

ISLE OF MAN. *View from the Top of Black Comb.*
——— *Epistle to Sir G. H. Beaumont.*
——— *Summer Tour*, 1833, XVI., XVII., XVIII., XIX.

PEELE CASTLE. *Elegiac Stanzas, Peele Castle.*

RUSHEN ABBEY, Bala-Sala. *Summer Tour*, 1833, XX.—*At Bala Sala.*

SNAFELL. *Summer Tour*, 1833, XXI. — *Tynwald Hill.*

TYNWALD HILL. *Summer Tour*, 1833, XXI. — *Tynwald Hill.*

V. Scotland.

" O'er hilly path, and open Strath,
We'll wander Scotland thorough."
— *Yarrow Unvisited.*

ABERDEEN. *Peter Bell*, Pt. I.
AILSA CRAG, off Ayrshire. *Summer Tour*, 1833, XXIII.—*In the Frith of Clyde.*

DUNOLLIE CASTLE, near Oban, Argyllshire. *Eagles. Composed at Dunollie Castle.*
—— *Summer Tour,* 1833, XXV.—*On revisiting Dunollie Castle.*

EDINBURGH.   *The Excursion,* Book IV., l. 913.
EILDON HILL, Roxburghshire. *Yarrow Revisited.*
—— *On the Departure of Sir Walter Scott from Abbotsford.*
E L L I S L A N D [Burns's residence], Dumfriesshire. *Thoughts suggested on the Banks of the Nith.*
ESK, RIVER, Dumfriesshire. *The Borderers,* Act I.
ETIVE GLEN, LOCH, Argyllshire. *Composed in the Glen of Loch Etive.*
—— *In the Sound of Mull.*
ETTRICK, Selkirkshire. *Effusion upon the Death of James Hogg.*

FIFESHIRE. *Peter Bell,* Pt. III.
FINLARIG, near Killin, Perthshire. *The Earl of Breadalbane's Ruined Mansion.*
FORTH, RIVER, Stirlingshire. *Yarrow Unvisited.*

GALLA WATER, RIVER, Edinburghshire. *Yarrow Unvisited.*
GARRY, RIVER, Perthshire. *Descriptive Sketches.*
—— *In the Pass of Killicranky.*
GLEN ALMOND, Perthshire. *Glen-Almain.*
GLENCROE, Argyllshire. *"'Rest and be thankful.'"*
GREENOCK, Renfrewshire. *Summer Tour,* 1833, XXXVI.—*Greenock.*

HAMILTON PALACE, Lanarkshire. *Picture of Daniel in the Lions' Den.*

INVERNESS, Inverness-shire. *Peter Bell,* Pt. I.
INVERSNEYD, Loch Lomond. *To a Highland Girl.*
—— *The Three Cottage Girls.*

NEIDPATH CASTLE, near PEEBLES.   *Composed at Neidpath Castle.*

NEWARK CASTLE, Ayrshire.   *Yarrow Visited.*

────── *Yarrow Revisited.*

NITH, RIVER, Dumfriesshire.   *Thoughts suggested on the Banks of the Nith.*

ROSLIN, Edinburghshire.   *"From the dark chambers of dejection freed."*

ROSLIN CHAPEL, Edinburghshire.   *Composed in Roslin Chapel.*

ST KILDA, ISLAND OF (Hebrides).   *Summer Tour,* 1833, XXXV.

ST MARY'S LAKE, Selkirkshire.   *Yarrow Unvisited.*

────── *Yarrow Visited.*

SCOTLAND.   *Descriptive Sketches.*

SELKIRK.   *Yarrow Unvisited.*

STAFFA, CAVE OF, Hebrides.   *Summer Tour,* 1833, XXVIII., XXIX., XXX., XXXI.

STIRLING CASTLE, Stirlingshire.   *Yarrow Unvisited.*

TAY, RIVER, Perthshire.   *Yarrow Unvisited.*

TIVIOTDALE, Roxburghshire.   *Yarrow Unvisited.*

TIVIOT, RIVER, Roxburghshire.   *Yarrow Revisited.*

────── *View from the Top of Black Comb.*

TROSSACHS, THE, Perthshire.   *The Trossachs.*

TWEED, RIVER, Peeblesshire. *Composed at* ────── *Castle.*

────── *Yarrow Unvisited.*

────── *The White Doe of Rylstone,* Canto III.

────── *Yarrow Revisited.*

────── *View from the Top of Black Comb.*

────── *Tour in Italy,* 1837, I.—*Musings near Aquapendente.*

TYNDRUM, Perthshire.   *Suggested at Tyndrum.*

VOIL, LOCH, Perthshire.   *Rob Roy's Grave.*

YARROW, Selkirkshire. *Yarrow Unvisited.*

YARROW, VALE OF, Selkirkshire. *Yarrow Unvisited.*

—— *Yarrow Visited.*

—— *Yarrow Revisited.*

YARROW, RIVER, Selkirkshire. *The Force of Prayer.*

—— *Effusion upon the Death of James Hogg.*

—— *Yarrow Unvisited.*

—— *Yarrow Visited.*

—— *Yarrow Revisited.*

—— *Summer Tour,* 1833, XLVI.—*The Somnam-bulist.*

VI. IRELAND.

" Erin's Isle."
—*Malham Cove.*

FAIR HEAD, County Antrim. *Eagles (" Dishonoured rock and ruin ").*

GIANT'S CAUSEWAY, Antrim, Ireland. *Malham Cove.*

VII. THE CONTINENT, &C., OF EUROPE.

" I travelled among unknown men,
In lands beyond the sea."
—*" I travelled among."*

" All that I saw returns upon my view, ...
And where the foot with no unmanly fear
Recoiled—and wings alone could travel—there
I move at ease ; . . . . crossing the career
Of recollections vivid as the dreams
Of midnight,—cities, plains, forests, and mighty streams."
—*Desultory Stanzas.*

" Treasures I gained with zeal that neither feared
The toils nor felt the crosses of the way."
—*Memorials of Tour in Italy : To H. C. Robinson.*

AAR, RIVER (Handec), Switzerland. *Tour on Con-tinent,* 1820, XII.—*The Fall of the Aar.*

ACADEME, Greece. *Dion.*

ADRIATIC SEA, Italy.   *The Prelude*, Book VIII., l. 176.

AIX-LA-CHAPELLE, Prussia.   *Tour on Continent*, 1820, VI.—*Aix-la-Chapelle.*

ALBAN HILLS, Italy.   *Tour in Italy*, 1837, XI.—*From the Alban Hills.*

ALBANO, Italy.   *Tour in Italy*, 1837, IX.—*At Albano.*

ALBANO, ILEX-GROVE OF VILLA DORIA.   *Tour in Italy*, 1837, IX.—*At Albano.*

ALLONVILLE, France.   *The Poet's Dream.*

ALPS, THE, Switzerland.   *Peter Bell*, Prologue.

——— *Song for the Wandering Jew.*

——— *The Prelude*, Book VI., l. 591.

——— *To* ———, *on her ascent of Helvellyn.*

——— *"Advance — come forth from thy Tyrolean ground."*

——— *Tour on Continent*, 1820, XXXVII.—*Desultory Stanzas.*

ALTORF, TELL'S TOWER AT (Switzerland),   *Tour on Continent*, 1820, XIX.—*Effusion.*

ALVERNIAC ("Laverna").   *Tour in Italy*, 1837, XIV.—*The Cuckoo at Laverna.*

ANIO, RIVER, Italy.   *Tour on Continent*, 1820, XXIX.—*Stanzas.*

——— *Tour in Italy*, 1837, X.

ANTIPAROS, GROTTO OF (Isle of Cyclades, Greece).   *The Prelude*, Book VIII., l. 562.

AOSTA, Turin, N. Italy.   *Descriptive Sketches.*

APENNINES, THE, Italy.   *Tour in Italy*, 1837, I.—*Musings near Aquapendente.*

——— *Tour in Italy*, 1837, XIV.—*The Cuckoo at Laverna.*

AQUAPENDENTE, Italy.   *Tour in Italy*, 1837, I.—*Musings near Aquapendente.*

AQUITAINE, ancient province of France.   *Ecclesiastical Sonnets*, Pt. I., xxxiv.

CADENABBIA, N. Italy. *Tour on Continent*, 1820, XXV.—*The Italian Itinerant and the Swiss Goatherd*, Pt. I., iii.

CALAIS, France. *Composed by the Sea-side, near Calais.*

——— *Calais, August* 1802.

——— *Composed near Calais.*

——— *Calais, August* 15, 1802.

——— *Composed on the Beach near Calais.*

——— *September* 1, 1802 (" *We had a female passenger* ").

——— *Tour on Continent*, 1820, I.—*Fish-Women.*

CALATERIUM, ancient city of France (?) *Artegal and Elidure.*

CALPE, CLIFFS OF, Valencia, Spain. *The Excursion*, Book IX., l. 336.

CAMADOLI, CONVENT OF, Italy. *Tour in Italy*, 1837, XV. and XVI.—*At the Convent of Camaldoli.*

——— UPPER CONVENT OF, *Tour in Italy*, 1837, xvii.—*At the Eremite.*

CAMPANIA, division of Italy. *Tour in Italy*, 1837, I. —*Musings near Aquapendente.*

CASTALY, a spring at the foot of Parnassus, Greece. " *Pelion and Ossa flourish side by side.*"

CEPHISUS, RIVER, Greece. *The Excursion*, Book IV., ll. 749-757.

CHAMBORD, near Blois, France. *The Prelude*, Book IX., l. 491.

CHAMOUNY, valley of France, in Savoy. *Descriptive Sketches.*

——— *The Prelude*, Book VI., ll. 528-533.

——— *Tour on Continent*, 1820, XXXI.—*Processions.*

CHARTREUSE, GRANDE, Monastery in France. *Descriptive Sketches.*

——— *The Prelude*, Book VI., l. 418.

CHARTREUSE, ROCK OF, France. *The Prelude*, Book VIII., l. 274.

FLORENCE, Italy.   *Tour in Italy,* 1837, XXI., XXII.
—*At Florence.*
———— *Tour in Italy,* 1837, XIX.—*At Florence.*
FLORENCE, DANTE'S SEAT (" Sasso di Dante ") at.
Tour in Italy, 1837, XIX.— *At Florence.*
FLORENCE, TRIBUNA.   *Tour in Italy,* 1837, XX.—
Before the Picture of the Baptist.
FORT FUENTES, head of Lake Como, N. Italy.
Tour on Continent, 1820, XXII.—*Fort Fuentes.*
FOURCHES, LES, Switzerland.   *Tour on Continent,*
1820, XXXVII.—*Desultory Stanzas.*

FRANCE.   *Descriptive Sketches.*

GALESUS, RIVER, Italy.   *The Prelude,* Book VIII.,
l. 175.
GEMMI, THE, Pass in Italy.   *Tour on Continent,* 1820,
XXX.—*Stanzas.*
GIBRALTAR, Spain.   *Suggested by a Portrait.*
GOLDAU, Switzerland.   *Tour on Continent,* 1820,
XXXII.—*Elegiac Stanzas.*
GOSLAR, Germany.   *The Prelude,* Book I., l. 7 ; VII.,
l. 3 ; VIII., ll. 210-211.
GOTHA, Germany.   *Installation Ode,* 1847.
GRAVEDONA, N. Italy.   *The Prelude,* Book VI., l.
700.
GUERNICA, Spain.   *The Oak of Guernica.*

HEIDELBERG, CASTLE OF, Germany.   *Tour on Con-*
tinent, 1820, IX.—*Hymn for the Boatmen.*
HELLESPONT, THE.   *Laodamia.*
HERCYNIAN FOREST, Germany.   *The Prelude,* Book
VIII., l. 215.
HOCHHEIM, Prussia.   *The Germans on the Heights of*
Hochheim.

IDA, MOUNT, Greece.   *The Triad.*

JULIAN [or CARNIC] ALPS. *Tour on Continent,* 1820, XXVI.—*The Eclipse of the Sun.*
JUNG-FRAU, mountain of Switzerland. *Ecclesiastical Sonnets,* Pt. II., xliii.
——— *Tour on Continent,* 1820, XXXVII.—*Desultory Stanzas.*

LAGO MORTO, Italy. *Tour in Italy,* 1837, XXV.—*After leaving Italy.*
LEINE, RIVER, Germany. *Installation Ode,* 1847.
LEMNOS, ISLE OF, island of Turkey. " *When Philoctetes in the Lemnian isle.*"
LOIRE, RIVER, France. *The Prelude,* Book IX., l. 41, 425, 431 ; Book X., l. 6.
LOIRET, France. *Descriptive Sketches.*
LOMBARDY, Italy. *Tour in Italy,* 1837, XXIV.—*In Lombardy.*
LUCERNE, Switzerland. *Tour on Continent,* 1820, XXXII.—*Elegiac Stanzas.*
LUCERNE CATHEDRAL, Switzerland. *Tour on Continent,* 1820, XXXVII.—*Desultory Stanzas.*
LUCERNE, LAKE, Switzerland. *Composed at Cora Linn.*
——— *Tour on Continent,* 1820, XXXVII.—*Desultory Stanzas.*
LUCRETILIS, a mountain in Italy. *The Prelude,* Book VIII., l. 182.
LUGANO, Switzerland. *Descriptive Sketches.*
LUGANO, LAKE, Switzerland. *Tour on Continent,* 1820, XXVI.—*The Eclipse of the Sun.*
——— *Tour on Continent,* 1820, XXVII.—*The Three Cottage Girls,* VI.

MADEIRA, Spain. *To a Lady* ("*Fair Lady! can I sing*").
MAGGIORE, LAKE, Switzerland. *The Prelude,* Book VI., ll. 655-658.

MAGGIORE, LAKE ("Locarno's Lake"). *Dion* (early edd).

MÆNALUS, a mountain in Arcadia. *Dion.*

MAMERTINUS, CARCER [" Mamertine Prison "]. *Tour in Italy,* 1837, I—*Musings near Aquapendente.*

MARATHON, PLAIN OF, Greece. *Composed at Cora Linn.*

MEUSE, RIVER, France. *Tour on Continent,* 1820, V. —*Between Namur and Liege.*

MILAN, N. Italy. *Tour on Continent,* 1820, XXVI.— *The Eclipse of the Sun.*

MILAN, DA VINCI'S "LAST SUPPER" IN CONVENT OF MARIA DELLA GRAZIA. *Tour on Continent,* 1820, XXV.—*The Last Supper.*

MONTE AMIATA, hill of Italy. *Tour in Italy,* 1837, I.—*Musings near Aquapendente.*

MONT BLANC, France. *The Prelude,* Book VI., l. 525.

MONTE CARLO (" Monte Calvo "). *Tour in Italy,* 1837, IX.—*At Albano.*

MONTE ROSA, Switzerland. *Ecclesiastical Sonnets,* Pt. III., 46.

MOSCOW, Russia. *The French Army in Russia.*
———— *The Russian Fugitive,* Pt. I., IV.
———— THE KREMLIN. *The Russian Fugitive,* Pt. III.

NAPLES (" Soft Parthenope "), Italy. *On the Departure of Sir Walter Scott from Abbotsford.*
———— *Tour in Italy,* 1837, I.—*Musings.*

NAPLES, BAY OF. *Tour in Italy,* 1837, I.—*Musings near Aquapendente.*

NYSA, ISLE OF (Legendary Scene associated with Bacchus). *The Brownie's Cell,* X.

OLYMPUS, mountain of Thessaly. " *Pelion and Ossa flourish side by side.*"

ORLEANS, France. *The Prelude*, Book IX., ll. 40-41 ;
X., ll. 94-96.
OSSA, mountain in Greece. " *Pelion and Ossa flourish
side by side.*"

PÆSTUM, ruined city of Italy. *Tour on Continent*,
1820, XXIX.—*Stanzas.*
PARIS. *The Prelude*, Book IX., ll. 42-214 ; X., ll. 11,
48-93.
——— *Ecclesiastical Sonnets*, Pt. II., xlii.
——— NOTRE DAME CHURCH. *The Poet's Dream.*
PARNASSUS, mountain in Greece. " *Pelion and Ossa
flourish side by side.*"
——— *Tour on Continent*, 1820, XXXVII.—*Desultory
Stanzas.*
PARTHENOPE [NAPLES]. *Tour in Italy*, 1837, I.—
Musings near Aquapendente.
PELION, mountain in Greece. " *Pelion and Ossa
flourish side by side.*"
PERMESSUS, river of Boeotia. *Epitaphs from Chiabrera,*
V. IX.
PIEDMONT, Italy. *Descriptive Sketches.*
PINDUS, mountains in Turkey. *To the Torrent at the
Devil's Bridge.*
PISA, CAMPO SANTO (Italy). *Tour in Italy*, 1837, I.—
Musings near Aquapendente.
PISA CATHEDRAL (Italy). *Tour in Italy*, 1837, I.—
Musings near Aquapendente.
POICTIERS, France. *Yew Trees.*
——— *Ecclesiastical Sonnets*, Pt. II., xvi.
POMPEII, ruined city of Italy. *Tour on Continent*,
1820, XXIX.—*Stanzas.*
PO, RIVER, Italy. *Ecclesiastical Sonnets*, Pt. II., xiii.
——— *Tour on Continent*, 1820, XIV.—*Composed in
one of the Catholic Cantons.*
POSILIPO, SCUOLA DI VIRGILIO, near. *Tour in Italy*,
1837, I.—*Musings near Aquapendente.*

RADICOFANI, mountain in Italy. *Tour in Italy*, 1837, I.—*Musings near Aquapendente.*

REUSS, RIVER, canton Uri, Switzerland. *Descriptive Sketches.*

RHINE, RIVER. *Descriptive Sketches.*
———— *The Prelude*, Book IX., l. 184.
———— *The Excursion*, Book VII., l. 788.
———— *The Germans on the Heights of Hochheim.*
———— *Ecclesiastical Sonnets*, Pt. II., xliii.; III., xii.
———— *Tour on Continent*, 1820, XIV.—*Composed in one of the Catholic Cantons.*
———— *Tour on Continent*, 1820: *Author's Voyage down the Rhine* (edn. 1822).
———— *Tour on Continent*, 1820, VIII.—*In a Carriage upon the Banks of the Rhine.*
———— *Tour on Continent*, 1820, IX.—*Hymn for the Boatmen.*
———— *A Jewish Family.*
———— *To the Torrent at the Devil's Bridge.*
———— *Installation Ode*, 1847.

RHONE, RIVER, Switzerland and France. *The Prelude*, Book VI., l. 378.
———— *Tour on Continent*, 1820, XXXVII.—*Desultory Stanzas.*
———— *Ecclesiastical Sonnets*, Pt. II., xi.

RIGHI, MOUNT, Switzerland. *Tour on Continent*, 1820, XVIII.—*Our Lady of the Snow.*
———— *Tour on Continent*, 1820, XXXII.—*Elegiac Stanzas.*

ROME, Italy. *The Prelude*, Book VII., l. 80.
———— *Spanish Guerillas.*
———— *The Eagle and the Dove.*
———— *The Pillar of Trajan.*
———— *Tour on Continent*, 1820, XXIX.—*Stanzas.*
———— *Tour in Italy*, 1837, I.—*Musings near Aquapendente.*
———— *Tour in Italy*, 1837, II., III., IV., V., VII., VIII.

ROME, Italy. *Tour in Italy*, 1837, XII. — *Near Lake Thrasymene.*

—————— " *Why should we weep or mourn.*"

—————— COLISEUM. *Composed at Rydal on May Morning.*

—————— JANICULAR MOUNT. *Tour in Italy*, 1837, I. —*Musings near Aquapendente.*

—————— MONS PINCIUS. *Tour in Italy*, 1837, II.— *Pine of Monte Mario.*

—————— MONTE MARIO. *Tour in Italy*, 1837, II.— *Pine of Monte Mario.*

—————— ST PETER'S. *Tour in Italy*, 1837, II.—*Pine of Monte Mario.*

—————— —————— *Tour in Italy*, 1837, VIII. — *Near Rome.*

—————— —————— *The Poet's Dream.*

—————— TARPEIAN ROCK. *Tour in Italy*, 1837, III. —*At Rome.*

ROMORENTIN, France. *The Prelude*, Book IX., l. 481.

ROSA, MONTE, Switzerland. *Tour on Continent*, 1820, XXXVII.—*Desultory Stanzas.*

ROUEN, ST OUEN'S CHURCH. *The Poet's Dream.*

ST DENNIS, ABBEY CHURCH, France. *The Poet's Dream.*

ST GOTHARD, PASS OF, Switzerland. *Tour on Continent*, 1820, XXI.—*On Hearing the "Ranz des Vaches."*

ST MAURICE, France. *Tour on Continent*, 1820, XXXVII.—*Desultory Stanzas.*

SANGUINETTO, small river of Italy. *Tour in Italy*, 1837, XII., XIII.

SAN SALVADOR, CHURCH OF, Switzerland. *Tour on Continent*, 1820, XXIII.—*Church of San Salvador.*

SAONE, RIVER, France. *The Prelude*, Book VI., l. 376.

SARNEN, MOUNT, Switzerland. *Tour on Continent,* 1820, XXXVII.—*Desultory Stanzas.*

SARAGOSSA ("Zaragoza"). *"And is it among rude untutored Dales."*
———— *"Hail Zaragoza ! If with unwet eye."*

SAVONA, Italy. *Epitaphs from Chiabrera,* III., V., VIII.
———— *Tour in Italy,* 1837, I.—*Musings near Aquapendente.*

SCHAFFHAUSEN, FALL OF, Switzerland. *Ecclesiastical Sonnets,* Pt. II., xliii.

SCHWYTZ, Switzerland. *Tour on Continent,* 1820, XX. —*The Town of Schwytz.*

SCKELLENEN-THAL, Switzerland. *Descriptive Sketches.*

SEINE, RIVER, France. *Descriptive Sketches.*
———— *Ode ("Who rises on the banks of Seine"),* I.

SIMPLON PASS, Switzerland. *The Simplon Pass.*
———— *The Prelude,* Book VI., l. 563, and ll. 621-640.
———— COLUMN IN, Switzerland. *Tour on Continent,* 1820, XXVIII.—*Column intended for an edifice.*

SORRENTO, Italy. *Yarrow Revisited.*

STAUB-BACH, Lauterbrunnen (Switzerland). *Tour on Continent,* 1820, XI.—*On approaching the Staubbach.*

STOLBERG, Prussia. *The Armenian Lady's Love.*

SYRACUSE, town in Sicily. *The Prelude,* Book XI., l. 378.
———— *The Excursion,* Book VIII., l. 221.
———— *Dion.*

TEMPE, VALE OF, Greece. *By the side of Rydal Mere.*

THERMOPYLÆ, PASS OF, Greece. *Composed at Cora Linn.*

THESSALY, Greece. *Dion.*

THRASYMENE, Italy. *Tour in Italy*, 1837, XII., XIII.—*Near Lake Thrasymene.*

THUN, Switzerland. *Tour on Continent*, 1820, XIII. —*Memorial.*

TIBER, RIVER, Italy. *Ecclesiastical Sonnets*, Pt. II., xxvii.

TROY, ancient city of Greece. *Laodamia.*

TUSA, RIVER, Switzerland? *Descriptive Sketches.*

TUSCULUM, ancient town of Italy. *Tour in Italy*, 1837, I.—*Musings near Aquapendente.*

UNDERWALDEN, Switzerland. *Descriptive Sketches.*

URI, canton of Switzerland. *Tour on Continent*, 1820, XXVII.—*The Three Cottage Girls.*

URI, LAKE, Switzerland. *Descriptive Sketches.*

URSEREN, VALE OF, Switzerland. *Descriptive Sketches.*

VALLAIS, Switzerland. *The Prelude*, Book VI., l. 562.

VALLOMBRE VALLEY, France. *The Prelude*, Book VI., l. 480.

VALLOMBROSA, TUSCAN ABBEY, Italy. *Tour on Continent*, 1820, XXIX.—*Stanzas.*

VALLOMBROSA, Italy. *Tour in Italy*, 1837, XVIII. —*At Vallombrosa.*

—————— MONASTERY OF. *Tour in Italy*, 1837, XVIII. —*At Vallombrosa.*

VANNES, France. *The Eagle and the Dove.*

VENICE, Italy. *On the extinction of the Venetian Republic.*

—————— *Ecclesiastical Sonnets*, Pt. II., xiii.

—————— *The Armenian Lady's Love.*

—————— *Tour in Italy*, 1837, XXV.—*After Leaving Italy.*

VESUVIUS, S. Italy. *Yarrow Revisited.*

VIA MALA, Grisons, Switzerland. *Descriptive Sketches.*

VIA MALA, Switzerland. *To the Torrent at the Devil's Bridge.*

VIENNA, Austria. *Siege of Vienna raised by John Sobieski.*

WATERLOO, Belgium. *Occasioned by the Battle of Waterloo.*
——— *Tour on Continent,* 1820, IV.—*After Visiting Waterloo.*

ZACYNTHUS, island in Ionian Sea. *The Prelude,* Book IX., l. 416.

ZARAGOZA [=Saragossa]. *"And is it among rude untutored Dales."*
——— ——— *"Hail Zaragoza! 'If with unwet eye."*

ZURICH, LAKE, Switzerland. *Tour on Continent,* 1820, XXXII.—*Elegiac Stanzas.*

ZUTPHEN, Holland. *Descriptive Sketches.*

VIII. ASIA.

" Syria's marble ruins towering high
 Above the sandy desert."
   —*The Excursion,* Book III.

" Tyre, by the margin of the sounding waves,
 Palmyra, central in the desert."
   —*The Excursion,* Book VIII.

" Siberian snows."
   —*Peter Bell.*

AGRA, India. *The Prelude,* Book X., l. 19.
ANDES, Mountains. *Peter Bell,* Prologue.
ARABIA. *Ecclesiastical Sonnets,* Part II., xxvii.

BABYLON, ancient city of Chaldea. *The Prelude,* Book VII., l. 81.

NAZARETH, Galilee, Palestine. *Ecclesiastical Sonnets,* Pt. I., xxxiii.
NIPHATES, mountain in Asia. *To ——, on her ascent of Helvellyn.*

PALESTINE. *The Borderers,* Act III.
PALMYRA, ancient city of Syria. *The Excursion,* Book III., ll. 150-152; VIII., l. 218.
PERSEPOLIS, ancient capital of Persia, Asia. *The Prelude,* Book VII., l. 81.
—— *Tour on Continent,* 1820, XXXI.—*Processions.*

SIBERIA, Asia. *The French Army in Russia.*
SILOA, BROOK, Palestine. *Ecclesiastical Sonnets,* Pt. II., xlvi.
SINAI, mountain in Arabia. *Tour on Continent,* 1820, XXIII.—*Church of San Salvador.*
—— *Ecclesiastical Sonnets,* Pt. II., xlvi.
SION. *Tour in Italy,* 1837, XVIII.—*At Vallombrosa.*
SYRIA. *The Borderers,* Act III.

TYRE, ancient city of Phœnicia. *The Excursion,* Book VIII., l. 217.
—— *Ecclesiastical Sonnets,* Pt. I., xxv.
—— *Translation of part of the Eneid,* Book I.

IX. AFRICA.

" Burning Africa."
—Peter Bell: Prologue.

AFRICA. *Peter Bell,* Prologue.
ALCAIRO [= Memphis (Egypt)]. *The Prelude,* Book VII., l. 81.

ATLAS, mountains in N. Africa. *Translation of part of the Eneid*, Book I.

CARTHAGE, ancient city of N. Africa. *Tour in Italy,* 1837, XII.—*Near Lake Thrasymene.*
———— *Translation of part of the Eneid,* Book I.

LIBYA, Africa. *Peter Bell*, Prologue.

MEMPHIS, ancient city of Egypt. *Ecclesiastical Sonnets*, Pt. I., xxv.

NIGER, RIVER, W. Africa. *The Excursion*, Book III., ll. 261-262.
NILE, RIVER, Egypt. *The Prelude*, Book VI., l. 614.
———— *Ecclesiastical Sonnets*, Pt. II., xxvii; III., xxxviii.

THEBES, city of Ancient Egypt. *The Excursion*, Book VIII., l. 216.

X. AMERICA.

" The Western World."
—" Men of the Western World! in Fate's dark book."

ANDES, THE, S. America. *To* ——, *on her ascent of Helvellyn.*

HUDSON, RIVER, U.S.A. *The Excursion*, Book III., ll. 881-884.

MISSISSIPPI, RIVER, U.S.A. *The Excursion*, Book III., l. 931.

New York, U.S.A.   *The Excursion*, Book III., ll. 884-885.

Ontario, Canada.   *The River Duddon*, XIII.

Oroonoko, River, S. America.   *The River Duddon*, XVI.

St Lawrence, River, N. America.   *The Excursion*, Book III., ll. 931-932.

FAMILIAR QUOTATIONS

FROM

WORDSWORTH.

" Since Milton, I know of no poet with so many felicities *and unforgetable lines and stanzas as you."*
—Letter of S. T. Coleridge to Wordsworth, in Christopher Wordsworth's Memoirs of Wordsworth.—Vol. II., pp. 74-75.

" Of no other poet, except Shakespeare, have so many phrases become household words as of Wordsworth."
—James Russell Lowell : Essay on Wordsworth.

FAMILIAR QUOTATIONS

FROM

WORDSWORTH.

" Happy the feeling from the bosom thrown
In perfect shape (whose beauty Time shall spare
Though a breath made it) like a bubble blown
For summer pastime into wanton air;
Happy the thought best likened to a stone
Of the sea-beach, when, polished with nice care,
Veins it discovers exquisite and rare,
Which for the loss of that moist gleam atone
That tempted first to gather it."
   —To ——. ("Happy the feeling.")

NOTE.—The following collection of Familiar Quotations from Wordsworth is arranged in the chronological order of the composition of the Poems from which they are taken. The year to which each one belongs is appended on the left hand of the page, and directly under each passage. The numbers of the quotations are given to facilitate reference from the Index. The references to the series to which the poems belong refer to the Poet's last editions, and to the editions published since his death by Messrs Moxon and Messrs Ward, Lock & Co. The name of each series of Poems I have abbreviated as shown in the Prefatory Note to the " List of Wordsworth's Best Poems."

1. O glide, fair stream! for ever so,
   Thy quiet soul on all bestowing,
   Till all our minds for ever flow
   As thy deep waters now are flowing.
(1789)   *—Remembrance of Collins.*
                        (POEMS: YOUTH, V.)

2. To all that binds the soul in powerless trance,
　　Lip-dewing song, and ringlet-tossing dance.
(1793)　　　　　　　　—*Descriptive Sketches.*
　　　　　　　　　　(POEMS : YOUTH, VI.)

3. And homeless near a thousand homes I stood,
　　And near a thousand tables pined and wanted
　　　food.
(1793-94)　　　　　　—*Guilt and Sorrow*, XLI.
　　　　　　　　　　(POEMS : YOUTH, VIII.)

4. True dignity abides with him alone
　　Who, in the silent hour of inward thought,
　　Can still suspect, and still revere himself,
　　In lowliness of heart.
(1795)　　　　—*Lines left upon a seat in a yew tree.*
　　　　　　　　　　(POEMS : YOUTH, VII.)

5. Action is transitory—a step, a blow,
　　The motion of a muscle—this way or that—
　　'Tis done, and in the after-vacancy
　　We wonder at ourselves, like men betrayed.
　　Suffering is permanent, obscure and dark,
　　And shares the nature of infinity.
(1795-6)　　　　　　—*The Borderers*, Act III.

6. —— A simple Child,
　　That lightly draws its breath,
　　And feels its life in every limb,
　　What should it know of death ? *
(1798)　　　　　　　　—*We are Seven.*
　　　　　　　　　　(POEMS : CHILDHOOD; X.)

＊ This, the first verse of the poem, was added by Coleridge after the
composition of the succeeding verses.—ED.

7. O dearest, dearest boy! my heart
 For better lore would seldom yearn,
 Could I but teach the hundredth part
 Of what from thee I learn.
(1798)   *—Anecdote for Fathers.*
       (POEMS: CHILDHOOD, XII.)

8. O Reader! had you in your mind
 Such stores as silent thought can bring,
 O gentle reader! you would find
 A tale in every thing.
(1798)   *—Simon Lee.*
       (POEMS: SENTIMENT, &C., VI.)

9. I've heard of hearts unkind, kind deeds
 With coldness still returning ;
 Alas! the gratitude of men
 Hath oftener left me mourning.
(1798)   *—Simon Lee.*
       (POEMS: SENTIMENT, &C., VI.)

10. In that sweet mood when pleasant thoughts
 Bring sad thoughts to the mind.
(1798)   *—Lines written in Early Spring.*
       (POEMS: SENTIMENT, &C., III.)

11. And 'tis my faith that every flower
 Enjoys the air it breathes.
(1798)   *—Lines written in Early Spring.*
       (POEMS: SENTIMENT, &C., III.)

12. And listens like a three years' child.*
       —Coleridge's *Ancient Mariner*, I.

---

* This and the next quotation were contributed by Wordsworth to
Coleridge's poem.—ED.

13. And thou art long and lank and brown
    As is the ribbed Sea-sand.
                    Coleridge's *Ancient Mariner*, IV.

14. Books .   .   .   .
    .   .   the spirit breathed
    From dead men to their kind.
    (1798)   —*Expostulation and Reply*.
                    (POEMS: SENTIMENT, &C., I.)

15. Nor less I deem that there are Powers
    Which of themselves our minds impress;
    That we can feed this mind of ours
    In a wise passiveness.
    (1798)   —*Expostulation and Reply*.
                    (POEMS: SENTIMENT, &C., I.)

16. Come forth into the light of things,
    Let Nature be your teacher.
    (1798)   —*The Tables Turned*.
                    (POEMS: SENTIMENT, &c., II.)

17. Sweet is the lore which Nature brings;
    Our meddling intellect
    Mis-shapes the beauteous forms of things:—
    We murder to dissect.
    (1798)   —*The Tables Turned*.
                    (POEMS: SENTIMENT, &c., II.)

18. One impulse from a vernal wood
    May teach you more of man,
    Of moral evil and of good,
    Than all the sages can.
    (1798)   —*The Tables Turned*
                    (POEMS: SENTIMENT, &c., II.)

19. The grass you almost hear it growing.
(1798)   —*The Idiot Boy.*
                    (POEMS: AFFECTIONS, XXXI.)

20. The bane of all that dread the devil!
(1798)   —*The Idiot Boy.*
                    (POEMS: AFFECTIONS, XXXI.)

21.   Sensations sweet,
    Felt in the blood, and felt along the heart.
(1798)   —*Tintern Abbey.*
                    (POEMS: IMAGINATION, XXVI.)

22. That best portion of a good man's life,
    His little, nameless, unremembered, acts
    Of kindness and of love.
(1798)   —*Tintern Abbey.*
                    (POEMS: IMAGINATION, XXVI.)

23.   That blessèd mood,
    In which the burthen of the mystery,
    In which the heavy and the weary weight
    Of all this unintelligible world,
    Is lightened.
(1798)   —*Tintern Abbey.*
                    (POEMS: IMAGINATION, XXVI.)

24. While with an eye made quiet by the power
    Of harmony, and the deep power of joy,
    We see into the life of things.
(1798)   —*Tintern Abbey.*
                    (POEMS: IMAGINATION, XXVI.)

25.   The fretful stir
    Unprofitable, and the fever of the world,
    Have hung upon the beatings of my heart.
(1798)   —*Tintern Abbey.*
                    (POEMS: IMAGINATION, XXVI.)

26.   Here I stand, not only with the sense
     Of present pleasure, but with pleasing thoughts
     That in this moment there is life and food
     For future years.
(1798)   —*Tintern Abbey.*
            (POEMS: IMAGINATION, XXVI.)

27.   The sounding cataract
     Haunted me like a passion : the tall rock,
     The mountain, and the deep and gloomy wood,
     Their colours and their forms, were then to me
     An appetite ; a feeling and a love,
     That had no need of a remoter charm,
     By thought supplied, nor any interest
     Unborrowed from the eye.
(1798)   —*Tintern Abbey.*
            (POEMS: IMAGINATION, XXVI.)

28.   Hearing oftentimes
     The still, sad music of humanity,
     Nor harsh nor grating, though of ample power
     To chasten and subdue.
(1798)   —*Tintern Abbey.*
            (POEMS: IMAGINATION, XXVI.)

29.   A sense sublime
     Of something far more deeply interfused,
     Whose dwelling is the light of setting suns,
     And the round ocean and the living air,
     And the blue sky, and in the mind of man :
     A motion and a spirit, that impels
     All thinking things, all objects of all thought,
     And rolls through all things.
(1798)   —*Tintern Abbey.*
            (POEMS: IMAGINATION, XXVI.)

30.   Nature never did betray
  The heart that loved her.
(1798)   —*Tintern Abbey.*
          (POEMS: IMAGINATION, XXVI.)

31. Nor greetings where no kindness is, nor all
  The dreary intercourse of daily life.
(1798)   —*Tintern Abbey.*
          (POEMS: IMAGINATION, XXVI.)

32.   Thy mind
  Shall be a mansion for all lovely forms,
  Thy memory be as a dwelling-place
  For all sweet sounds and harmonies.
(1798)   —*Tintern Abbey.*
          (POEMS: IMAGINATION, XXVI.)

33. Men who can hear the Decalogue,
  And feel no self-reproach.
(1798)   —*The Old Cumberland Beggar.*
          (POEMS: OLD AGE, I.)

34. As in the eye of Nature he has lived,
  So in the eye of Nature let him die!
(1798)   —*The Old Cumberland Beggar.*
          (POEMS: OLD AGE, I.)

35. The common growth of mother-earth
  Suffices me—her tears, her mirth,
  Her humblest mirth and tears.
(1798)   —*Peter Bell*, Prologue.
          (POEMS: IMAGINATION.)

36. A potent wand doth Sorrow wield;
    What spell so strong as guilty Fear!
    Repentance is a tender Sprite;
    If aught on earth have heavenly might,
    'Tis lodged within her silent tear.
    (1798)   —*Peter Bell*, Prologue.
                              (POEMS: IMAGINATION.)

37. Full twenty times was Peter feared
    For once that Peter was respected.
    (1798)   —*Peter Bell*, Part First.
                              (POEMS: IMAGINATION.)

38. Where deep and low the hamlets lie
    Beneath their little patch of sky
    And little lot of stars.
    (1798)   —*Peter Bell*, Part First.
                              (POEMS: IMAGINATION.)

39. A primrose by a river's brim
    A yellow primrose was to him,
    And it was nothing more.
    (1798)   —*Peter Bell*, Part First.
                              (POEMS: IMAGINATION.)

40. The soul of happy sound was spread.
    (1798)   —*Peter Bell*, Part First.
                              (POEMS: IMAGINATION.)

41. The soft blue sky did never melt
    Into his heart: he never felt
    The witchery of the soft blue sky.
    (1798)   —*Peter Bell*, Part First.
                              (POEMS: IMAGINATION.)

42. On a fair prospect some have looked
    And felt, as I have heard them say,
    As if the moving time had been
    A thing as steadfast as the scene
    On which they gazed themselves away.
(1798)   —*Peter Bell*, Part First.
                    (POEMS : IMAGINATION.)

43. There was a hardness in his cheek,
    There was a hardness in his eye,
    As if the man had fixed his face,
    In many a solitary place,
    Against the wind and open sky !
(1798)   —*Peter Bell*,* Part First.
                    (POEMS : IMAGINATION.)

44. One of those heavenly days that cannot die.
(1799)   —*Nutting. l. 3 .*
                    (POEMS : IMAGINATION, VI.)

45. Then, dearest Maiden, move along these shades
    In gentleness of heart ; with gentle hand
    Touch—for there is a spirit in the woods.
(1799)   —*Nutting.*
                    (POEMS : IMAGINATION, VI.)

46. She dwelt among the untrodden ways
    Beside the springs of Dove,
    A Maid whom there were none to praise,
    And very few to love :

* The first and second editions only of this poem contain the following oft-quoted stanza :—
    43A. Is it a party in a parlour ?
        Crammed just as they on earth were cramm'd—
        Some sipping punch, some sipping tea,
        But as you by their faces see,
        All silent, and all damn'd !

A violet by a mossy stone
Half hidden from the eye!
—Fair as a star, when only one
Is shining in the sky.

She lived unknown, and few could know
When Lucy ceased to be;
For she is in her grave, and, oh,
The difference to me!
(1799)   *—She dwelt among the untrodden ways.*
          (POEMS: AFFECTIONS, VIII.)

47. I travelled among unknown men
    In lands beyond the sea;
    Nor, England, did I know till then
    What love I bore to thee.
(1799)   *—I travelled among unknown men.*
          (POEMS: AFFECTIONS, IX.)

48. And her's shall be the breathing balm,
    And her's the silence and the calm
    Of mute insensate things.
(1799)   *—Three Years she grew in sun and shower.*
          (POEMS: IMAGINATION, X.)

49. The stars of midnight shall be dear
    To her; and she shall lean her ear
    In many a secret place
    Where rivulets dance their wayward round,
    And beauty born of murmuring sound
    Shall pass into her face.
(1799)   *—Three Years she grew in sun and shower.*
          (POEMS: IMAGINATION, X.)

50. One that would peep and botanize
    Upon his mother's grave.
(1799)   *—A Poet's Epitaph.*
          (POEMS: SENTIMENT, &c., VIII.)

51. A reasoning, self-sufficing thing,
    An intellectual All-in-all !
(1799)   *—A Poet's Epitaph.*
          (POEMS: SENTIMENT, &c., VIII.)

52. He murmurs near the running brooks
    A music sweeter than their own.
    He is retired as noontide dew,
    Or fountain in a noon-day grove ;
    And you must love him, ere to you
    He will seem worthy of your love.
    The outward shows of sky and earth,
    Of hill and valley, he has viewed ;
    And impulses of deeper birth
    Have come to him in solitude.
(1799)   *—A Poet's Epitaph.*
          (POEMS: SENTIMENT, &c., VIII.)

53. The harvest of a quiet eye
    That broods and sleeps on his own heart.
(1799)   *—A Poet's Epitaph.*
          (POEMS: SENTIMENT, &c., VIII.)

54. Yet, sometimes, when the secret cup
    Of still and serious thought went round,
    It seemed as if he drank it up—
    He felt with spirit so profound.
(1799)   *—Matthew.*
          (POEMS: SENTIMENT, &c., X.)

55. No check, no stay, this Streamlet fears:
    How merrily it goes !
    'Twill murmur on a thousand years
    And flow as now it flows.
(1799)   *—The Fountain.*
          (POEMS: SENTIMENT, &c., XII.)

56. My eyes are dim with chillish tears,
    My heart is idly stirred,
    For the same sound is in my ears
    Which in those days I heard.
(1799)   —*The Fountain.*
                (POEMS: SENTIMENT, &c., XII.)

57.   The wiser mind
    Mourns less for what age takes away
    Than what it leaves behind.
(1799)   —*The Fountain.*
                (POEMS: SENTIMENT, &c., XII.)

58.   They see
    A happy youth, and their old age
    Is beautiful and free.
(1799)   —*The Fountain.*
                (POEMS: SENTIMENT, &c., XII.)

59.   Often, glad no more,
    We wear a face of joy, because
    We have been glad of yore.
(1799)   —*The Fountain.*
                (POEMS: SENTIMENT, &c., XII.)

60.   A wide moor,
    —The sweetest thing that ever grew
    Beside a human door!
(1799)   —*Lucy Gray.*
                (POEMS: CHILDHOOD, IX.)

61. And many an endless, endless lake,
    With all its fairy crowds
    Of islands, that together lie
    As quietly as spots of sky
    Among the evening clouds.
(1799)   —*Ruth.*
                (POEMS: IMAGINATION, XXI.)

62.   A Youth to whom was given
    So much of earth—so much of heaven,
    And such impetuous blood.
(1799)   —*Ruth.*
                (POEMS: IMAGINATION, XXI.)

63. Until a man might travel twelve stout miles,
    Or reap an acre of his neighbour's corn.
(1800)   —*The Brothers.*
                (POEMS: AFFECTIONS, I.)

64. The thought of death sits easy on the man
    Who has been born and dies among the mountains.
(1800)   —*The Brothers.*
                (POEMS: AFFECTIONS, I.)

65.   Time
    Is a true friend to sorrow.
(1800)   —*The Brothers.*
                (POEMS: AFFECTIONS, I.)

66. A pleasurable feeling of blind love,
    The pleasure which there is in life itself.
(1800)   —*Michael.*
                (POEMS: AFFECTIONS, XXXII.)

67.   A child, more than all other gifts
    That earth can offer to declining man,
    Brings hope with it, and forward-looking thoughts.
(1800)   —*Michael.*
                (POEMS: AFFECTIONS, XXXII.)

68. Something between a hindrance and a help.
(1800)   —*Michael.*
                (POEMS: AFFECTIONS, XXXII.)

69. Feelings and emanations—things which were
    Light to the sun and music to the wind.
    (1800)   —*Michael.*
                    (POEMS: AFFECTIONS, XXXII.)

70. There is a comfort in the strength of love;
    'Twill make a thing endurable, which else
    Would overset the brain, or break the heart.
    (1800)   —*Michael.*
                    (POEMS: AFFECTIONS, XXXII.)

71.   Lady of the Mere,
    Sole-sitting by the shores of old romance.
    (1800)   —*A narrow girdle of rough stones and crags.*
                    (POEMS: PLACES, IV.)

72. The spot was made by Nature for herself.
    (1800)   —*To M. H.*
                    (POEMS: PLACES, V.)

73. He is oft the wisest man
    Who is not wise at all.
    (1800)   —*The Oak and the Broom*, vii.
                    (POEMS: FANCY, V.)

74. "A jolly place," said he, "in times of old!
    But something ails it now: the spot is curst."
    (1800)   —*Hart-leap Well*, Part Second.
                    (POEMS: IMAGINATION, XXIV.)

75. Hunt half a day for a forgotten dream.
    (1800)   —*Hart-leap Well*, Part Second.
                    (POEMS: IMAGINATION, XXIV.)

76. Never to blend our pleasure or our pride
   With sorrow of the meanest thing that feels.
(1800)   —*Hart-leap Well*, Part Second.
               (POEMS: IMAGINATION, XXIV.)

77. She gave me eyes, she gave me ears;
   And humble cares, and delicate fears;
   A heart, the fountain of sweet tears;
           And love, and thought, and joy.
(1801)   —*The Sparrow's Nest.*
               (POEMS: CHILDHOOD, III.)

78. O Cuckoo! shall I call thee Bird,
   Or but a wandering voice?
(1802)   —*To the Cuckoo* ("O blithe New-Comer.")
       (POEMS: IMAGINATION, II.)

79. The Child is father of the Man.
(1802)   —*My heart leaps up when I behold.*
           (POEMS: CHILDHOOD, I.)

80. The cattle are grazing,
   Their heads never raising;
   There are forty feeding like one!
(1802)   —*Written in March.*
           (POEMS: IMAGINATION, XVI.)

81. Sweet childish days, that were as long
   As twenty days are now.
(1802)   —*To a Butterfly* ("I've watched you.")
           (POEMS: AFFECTIONS, III.)

82. Pleasures newly found are sweet
   When they lie about our feet.
(1802)   —*To the Small Celandine* ("Pleasures newly
               found are sweet.")
           (POEMS: FANCY, XII.)

83. Often have I sighed to measure
    By myself a lonely pleasure,
    Sighed to think, I read a book,
    Only read, perhaps, by me.
(1802)   —*To the Small Celandine* ("Pleasures newly
                    found are sweet").
                (POEMS: FANCY, XII.)

84. As high as we have mounted in delight
    In our dejection do we sink as low.
(1802)   —*The Leech-Gatherer ; or, Resolution and
                    Independence*, iv.
                (POEMS: IMAGINATION, XXII.)

85. But how can he expect that others should
    Build for him, sow for him, and at his call
    Love him, who for himself will take no heed at all?
(1802)   —*The Leech-Gatherer ; or, Resolution and
                    Independence*, vi.
                (POEMS: IMAGINATION, XXII.)

86. I thought of Chatterton, the marvellous Boy,
    The sleepless Soul that perished in his pride ;
    Of Him who walked in glory and in joy
    Following his plough, along the mountain-side :
    By our own spirits are we deified :
    We Poets in our youth begin in gladness ;
    But thereof come in the end despondency and
    madness.
(1802)   *The Leech-Gatherer ; or, Resolution and
                    Independence*, vii.
                (POEMS: IMAGINATION, XXII.)

87. Motionless as a cloud   .   .   .   .
    That heareth not the loud winds when they call ;
    And moveth all together if it move at all.
(1802)   —*The Leech-Gatherer ; or, Resolution and
                    Independence*, xi.
                (POEMS: IMAGINATION, XXII.)

88. Choice word and measured phrase, above the reach
    Of ordinary men.
(1802)   —*The Leech-Gatherer ; or, Resolution and*
                        Independence, xiv.
            (POEMS : IMAGINATION, XXII.)

89. And mighty Poets in their misery dead.
(1802)   —*The Leech-Gatherer ; or, Resolution and*
                        Independence, xvii.
            (POEMS : IMAGINATION, XXII.)

90. Ne'er saw I, never felt, a calm so deep !
    The river glideth at his own sweet will :
    Dear God ! the very houses seem asleep ;
    And all that mighty heart is lying still !
(1802)   —*Sonnet, composed on Westminster Bridge.*
            (MISC. SONNETS, Pt. II., xxxvi.)

91. The holy time is quiet as a Nun
    Breathless with adoration.
(1802)   —*It is a beauteous evening, calm and free.*
            (MISC. SONNETS, Pt. I., xxx.)

92. Men are we, and must grieve when even the Shade
    Of that which once was great, is passed away.
(1802)   —*On the Extinction of the Venetian Republic.*
            (POEMS : TO LIBERTY, Pt. I., vi.)

93.   Thou hast left behind
    Powers that will work for thee ; air, earth, and
        skies ;
    There's not a breathing of the common wind
    That will forget thee ; thou hast great allies ;
    Thy friends are exultations, agonies,
    And love, and man's unconquerable mind.
(1802)   —*To Toussaint L'Ouverture.*
            (POEMS : TO LIBERTY, Pt. I., viii.)

94. Plain living and high thinking are no more:
    The homely beauty of the good old cause
    Is gone; our peace, our fearful innocence,
    And pure religion breathing household laws.
    (1802)   —*Written in London, Sept.* 1802.
                       (POEMS: TO LIBERTY, Pt. I., xiii.)

95. Thy soul was like a Star, and dwelt apart.
    (1802)   —*London,* 1802.
                       (POEMS: TO LIBERTY, Pt. I., xiv.)

96. So didst thou travel on life's common way,
    In cheerful godliness.
    (1802)   —*London,* 1802.
                       (POEMS: TO LIBERTY, Pt. I., xiv.)

97. We must be free or die, who speak the tongue
    That Shakespeare spake; the faith and morals hold
    Which Milton held.
    (1802)   —*It is not to be thought of.*
                       (POEMS: TO LIBERTY, Pt. I., xvi.)

98. But verse was what he had been wedded to;
    And his own mind did like a tempest strong
    Come to him thus, and drove the weary Wight
       along.
    (1802)   —*Stanzas Written in Thomson's " Castle of
                       Indolence."*
                       (POEMS: AFFECTIONS, V.)

99. A noticeable Man with large grey eyes.
    (1802)   —*Stanzas written in Thomson's " Castle of
                       Indolence."*
                       (POEMS: AFFECTIONS, V.)

100. Glasses he had, that little things display,
The beetle panoplied in gems and gold,
A mailèd angel on a battle day.
(1802)   —*Stanzas written in Thomson's " Castle of
Indolence."*
(POEMS : AFFECTIONS, V.)

101. And oft alone in nooks remote
We meet thee, like a pleasant thought,
When such are wanted.
(1802)   —*To the Daisy* (" In youth from rock
to rock ").
(POEMS : FANCY, VII.)

102. The Poet's darling.
(1802)   —*To the Daisy* (" In youth from rock
to rock ").
(POEMS : FANCY, VII.)

103. Thou unassuming Common-place
Of Nature.
(1802)   —*To the Daisy* (" With little here to do
or see ").
(POEMS : FANCY, VIII.)

104. Oft on the dappled turf at ease
I sit, and play with similes,
Loose types of things through all degrees.
(1802)   —*To the Daisy* (" With little here to do or
see ").
(POEMS : FANCY, VIII.)
H

105. Sweet Mercy! to the gates of Heaven
    This Minstrel lead, his sins forgiven ;
    The rueful conflict, the heart riven
        With vain endeavour,
    And Memory of Earth's bitter leaven
        Effaced for ever.
(1803) —*Thoughts suggested on the Banks of the*
            Nith.
        (TOUR IN SCOTLAND, 1803, III.)

106. The best of what we do and are,
        Just God, forgive !
(1803) —*Thoughts suggested on the Banks of the*
            Nith.
        (TOUR IN SCOTLAND, 1803, III.)

107. Thou art to me but as a wave
    Of the wild sea.
(1803)   —*To a Highland Girl.*
        (TOUR IN SCOTLAND, 1803, VI.)

108. A voice so thrilling ne'er was heard
    In spring-time from the Cuckoo-bird,
    Breaking the silence of the seas
    Among the farthest Hebrides.
(1803)   *The Solitary Reaper.*
        (TOUR IN SCOTLAND, 1803, IX.)

109. For old, unhappy, far-off things,
    And battles long ago.
(1803)   *The Solitary Reaper.*
        (TOUR IN SCOTLAND, 1803, IX.)

110. Some natural sorrow, loss, or pain,
    That has been, and may be again.
(1803)   —*The Solitary Reaper.*
        (TOUR IN SCOTLAND, 1803, IX.)

111. The music in my heart I bore,
 Long after it was heard no more.
(1803)   —*The Solitary Reaper.*
          (TOUR IN SCOTLAND, 1803, IX.)

112. Child of loud-throated War! the mountain Stream
 Roars in thy hearing; but thy hour of rest
 Is come, and thou art silent in thy age.
(1803)   —*Address to Kilchurn Castle.*
          (TOUR IN SCOTLAND, 1803, X.)

113. Yon foaming flood seems motionless as ice;
 Its dizzy turbulence eludes the eye,
 Frozen by distance.
(1803)   —*Address to Kilchurn Castle.*
          (TOUR IN SCOTLAND, 1803, X.)

114.   The good old rule
 Sufficeth them, the simple plan,
 That they should take who have the power,
 And they should keep who can.
(1803)   —*Rob Roy's Grave.*
          (TOUR IN SCOTLAND, 1803, XI.)

115. The Eagle, he was lord above,
 And Rob was lord below.
(1803)   —*Rob Roy's Grave.*
          (TOUR IN SCOTLAND, 1803, XI.)

116. A brotherhood of venerable Trees.
(1803)   *Sonnet, Composed at —— Castle.*
          (TOUR IN SCOTLAND, 1803, XII.)

117. Let beeves and home-bred kine partake
 The sweets of Burn-mill meadow;
 The swan on still St Mary's Lake
 Float double, swan and shadow!
(1803)   —*Yarrow Unvisited.*
          (TOUR IN SCOTLAND, 1803, XIII.)

118. A remnant of uneasy light,
     A flash of something over-bright!
(1803)   —*The Matron of Jedborough and her
                              husband.*
              (TOUR IN SCOTLAND, 1803, XV.)

119. Every gift of noble origin
     Is breathed upon by Hope's perpetual breath.
(1803)   —*October*, 1803 (" These times strike ").
              (POEMS TO LIBERTY, Pt. I., xx.)

120. O for a single hour of that Dundee
     Who on that day the word of onset gave!
(1803)   —*In the Pass of Killicranky.*
              (TOUR IN SCOTLAND, 1803, XIV.)

121. She was a Phantom of delight
     When first she gleamed upon my sight;
     A lovely apparition, sent
     To be a moment's ornament;
(1804)   —*She was a Phantom of delight.*
              (POEMS: IMAGINATION, VIII.)

122. But all things else about her drawn
     From May-time and the cheerful Dawn.
(1804)   —*She was a Phantom of delight.*
              (POËMS: IMAGINATION, VIII.)

123. A countenance in which did meet
     Sweet records, promises as sweet;
     A Creature not too bright or good
     For human nature's daily food;
     For transient sorrows, simple wiles,
     Praise, blame, love, kisses, tears, and smiles.
(1804)   —*She was a Phantom of delight.*
              (POEMS: IMAGINATION, VIII.)

124. The reason firm, the temperate will,
    Endurance, foresight, strength, and skill;
    A perfect Woman, nobly planned,
    To warn, to comfort, and command.
(1804)   *—She was a Phantom of delight.*
                (POEMS: IMAGINATION, VIII.)

125.   That inward eye
    Which is the bliss of solitude.
(1804)   *—I wandered lonely as a cloud.*
                (POEMS: IMAGINATION, XII.)

126.   Enjoyments dwell
    In the impenetrable cell
    Of the silent heart which Nature
    Furnishes to every creature.
(1804)   *—The Kitten and the Falling Leaves.*
                (POEMS: FANCY, XXXI.)

127. To be a Prodigal's Favourite—then, worse truth,
    A Miser's Pensioner—behold our lot!
    O Man, that from thy fair and shining youth
    Age might but take the things Youth needed not!
(1804)   *—To the Small Celandine* ("There is a
                flower.").
                (POEMS: OLD AGE, III.)

128. Stern Daughter of the Voice of God!
    O Duty! if that name thou love
    Who art a light to guide, a rod
    To check the erring, and reprove.
(1805)   *—Ode to Duty.*
            (POEMS: SENTIMENT, &c., XIX.)

129. Serene will be our days and bright,
    And happy will our nature be,
    When love is an unerring light,
    And joy its own security.
                    —*Ode to Duty.*
            (POEMS: SENTIMENT, &c., XIX.)

130. Stern Lawgiver! yet thou dost wear
    The Godhead's most benignant grace ;
    Nor know we anything so fair
    As is the smile upon thy face :
    Flowers laugh before thee on their beds
    And fragrance in thy footing treads ;
    Thou dost preserve the stars from wrong ;
    And the most ancient heavens, through Thee,
        are fresh and strong.
(1805)   —*Ode to Duty.*
            (POEMS: SENTIMENT, &c., XIX.)

131. Give unto me, made lowly wise,
    The spirit of self-sacrifice ;
    The confidence of reason give ;
    And in the light of truth thy Bondman let me
        live !
(1805)   —*Ode to Duty.*
            (POEMS: SENTIMENT, &c., XIX.)

132. There sometimes doth a leaping fish
    Send through the tarn a lonely cheer ;
    The crags repeat the raven's croak,
    In symphony austere.
(1805)   —*Fidelity.*
            (POEMS: SENTIMENT, &c., XVIII.)

133. The light that never was on sea or land,
    The consecration, and the Poet's dream.
(1805)   —*Elegiac Stanzas, suggested by a Picture of*
            Peele Castle.
        (ELEGIAC PIECES, VI.)

134. Elysian quiet, without toil or strife.
(1805)   —*Elegiac Stanzas, suggested by a Picture of*
            Peele Castle.
        (ELEGIAC PIECES, VI.)

135. A *silent* Poet.
(1805)   —*When to the attractions of the busy world.*
        (POEMS : PLACES, VI.)

136. Shalt show us how divine a thing
    A woman may be made.
(1805)   —*To a Young Lady.*
        (POEMS : IMAGINATION, XXXVI.)

137. But an old age serene and bright,
    And lovely as a Lapland night,
    Shall lead thee to thy grave.
(1805)   —*To a Young Lady.*
        (POEMS : IMAGINATION, XXXVI.)

138. A man too happy for mortality.
(1805)   *Vandracour and Julia.*
        (POEMS : AFFECTIONS, XXX.)

139.   You have been wretched ; yet
    The silver shower, whose reckless burthen weighs
    Too heavily upon the lily's head,
    Oft leaves a saving moisture at its root.
(1805)   *Vandracour and Julia.*
        (POEMS : AFFECTIONS, XXX.)

140. Dust as we are, the immortal spirit grows
　　　Like harmony in music.
(1799-1805)　　　—*The Prelude*, Book I., ll. 340-341.

141.　　　　　　　　The statue . . . .
　　　Of Newton with his prism and silent face,
　　　The marble index of a mind for ever
　　　Voyaging through strange seas of Thought, alone.
　　　　　　　—*The Prelude*, Book III., ll. 60-63.

142. Sweet Spenser, moving through his clouded
　　　　heaven,
　　　With the moon's beauty and the moon's soft
　　　　pace.
　　　　　　　—*The Prelude*, Book III., ll. 280-281.

143.　　　　　　　　Hope,
　　　That never set the pains against the prize.
　　　　　　　—*The Prelude*, Book III., ll. 595-596.

144. Honour misplaced, and Dignity astray.
　　　　　　　—*The Prelude*, Book III., l. 600.

145.　　　　　　　I made no vows, but vows
　　　Were then made for me.
　　　　　　　—*The Prelude*, Book IV., ll. 334-335.

146. When from our better selves we have too long
　　　Been parted by the hurrying world, and droop,
　　　Sick of its business, of its pleasures tired,
　　　How gracious, how benign is Solitude.
　　　　　　　—*The Prelude*, Book IV., ll. 354-357.

147.　　　　　　　Another morn
　　　Risen on mid-noon.
　　　　　　　—*The Prelude*, Book VI., ll. 197-198.

148. How bright a face is worn when joy of one
 Is joy for tens of millions.
(1799-1805) —*The Prelude*, Book VI., ll. 348-349.

149. Bliss was it in that dawn to be alive,
 But to be young was very Heaven!
  —*The Prelude*, Book XI., ll. 108-109.

150. The budding rose above the rose full blown.
  —*The Prelude*, Book XI., l. 121.

151.   There is
 One great society alone on earth:
 The noble Living and the noble Dead.
  —*The Prelude*, Book XI., ll. 393-395.

152.   By love subsists
 All lasting grandeur, by pervading love;
 That gone, we are as dust.
  —*The Prelude*, Book XIV., ll. 168-170.

153. The One who is thy choice of all the world.
  —*The Prelude*, Book XIV., l. 178.

154. Joy in widest commonalty spread.*
(1805)   —*The Recluse*, l. 771.

155.   Must hang
 Brooding above the fierce confederate storm
 Of sorrow, barricadoed evermore
 Within the walls of cities.
  —*The Recluse*, ll. 830-833.

* This and the two following quotations are taken from that portion of the poem which the poet gave in his preface to *The Excursion.* The whole of Book I. of the poem (all that was written) is now published (London : Macmillan & Co., 1888).

156. Descend, prophetic Spirit! that inspir'st
     The human Soul of universal earth
     Dreaming on things to come.
                              —*The Recluse*, ll. 836-838.

157. Who, doomed to go in company with Pain,
     And Fear, and Bloodshed, miserable train!
     Turns his necessity to glorious gain.
     (1806)   —*Character of The Happy Warrior.*
                        (POEMS: SENTIMENT, &c., XXI.)

158. Controls them and subdues, transmutes, bereaves
     Of their bad influence, and their good receives.
     (1806)   —*Character of The Happy Warrior.*
                        (POEMS: SENTIMENT, &c., XXI.)

159. But who, if he be called upon to face
     Some awful moment to which Heaven has joined
     Great issues, good or bad for human kind,
     Is happy as a Lover; and attired
     With sudden brightness, like a Man inspired.
     (1806)   —*Character of The Happy Warrior.*
                        (POEMS: SENTIMENT, &c., XXI.)

160. And, through the heat of conflict, keeps the law
     In calmness made, and sees what he foresaw.
     (1806)   —*Character of the Happy Warrior.*
                        (POEMS: SENTIMENT, &c., XXI.)

161. Whom neither shape of danger can dismay,
     Nor thought of tender happiness betray.
     (1806)   —*Character of the Happy Warrior.*
                        (POEMS: SENTIMENT, &c., XXI.)

162. And, while the mortal mist is gathering, draws
　　His breath in confidence of Heaven's applause.
(1806)　　　　—*Character of the Happy Warrior.*
　　　　　　　(POEMS: SENTIMENT, &c., XXI.)

163. In the broad open eye of the solitary sky.
(1806)　　　　　　　　—*Stray Pleasures.*
　　　　　　　　(POEMS: FANCY, XXIV.)
164.　　Pleasure is spread through the earth
　　In stray gifts to be claimed by whoever shall find.
(1806)　　　　　　　　—*Stray Pleasures.*
　　　　　　　　(POEMS: FANCY, XXIV.)

165. Like—but oh, how different!
(1806)　　　　—*Yes, it was the mountain echo.*
　　　　　　　(POEMS: IMAGINATION, XXIX.)

166. Maidens withering on the stalk.
(1806)　　　　　　—*Personal Talk,* i.
　　　　　　　(POEMS: SENTIMENT, &c., XIII.)

167.　　　　　　　　Sweetest melodies
　　Are those that are by distance made more sweet;
　　Whose mind is but the mind of his own eyes,
　　He is a Slave.
(1806)　　　　　　—*Personal Talk,* ii.
　　　　　　　(POEMS: SENTIMENT, &c., XIII.)

168. Dreams, books, are each a world; and books,
　　we know,
　　Are a substantial world, both pure and good:
　　Round these, with tendrils strong as flesh and
　　blood,
　　Our pastime and our happiness will grow.
(1806)　　　　　　—*Personal Talk,* iii.
　　　　　　　(POEMS: SENTIMENT, &c., XIII.)

169. The gentle Lady married to the Moor;
    And heavenly Una, with her milk-white lamb.
(1806)   —*Personal Talk*, iii.
                    (POEMS: SENTIMENT, &c., XIII.)

170. Blessings be with them—and eternal praise,
    Who gave us nobler loves, and nobler cares—
    The Poets, who on earth have made us heirs
    Of truth and pure delight by heavenly lays!
(1806)   —*Personal Talk*, iv.
                    (POEMS: SENTIMENT, &c., XIII.)

171. The world is too much with us: late and soon,
    Getting and spending, we lay waste our powers:
    Little we see in Nature that is ours.
(1806)   —*The World is too much with us.*
                    (MISC. SONNETS, Pt. I., xxxiii.)

172.   Great God! I'd rather be
    A Pagan suckled in a creed outworn;
    So might I, standing on this pleasant lea,
    Have glimpses that would make me less forlorn;
    Have sight of Proteus rising from the sea;
    Or hear old Triton blow his wreathèd horn.
(1806)   — *The world is too much with us.*
                    (MISC. SONNETS, Pt. I., xxxiii.)

173. A Power is passing from the earth.
(1806)   —*Lines Composed at Grasmere.*
                    (ELEGIAC PIECES, X.)

174.   But yet I know, where'er I go,
    That there hath passed away a glory from the
        earth.
(1803-6)   —*Ode. Intimations of Immortality*, II.

175. Our birth is but a sleep and a forgetting :
　　The Soul that rises with us, our life's Star,
　　　　Hath had elsewhere its setting,
　　　　　And cometh from afar :
　　　Not in entire forgetfulness,
　　　And not in utter nakedness,
　　But trailing clouds of glory do we come
　　　　From God, who is our home :
　　Heaven lies about us in our infancy !
(1803-6)　　—*Ode. Intimations of Immortality,* V.

176. At length the man perceives it die away,
　　And fade into the light of common day.
(1803-6)　　—*Ode. Intimations of Immortality,* V.

177. Haunted for ever by the eternal mind.
(1803-6)　　—*Ode. Intimations of Immortality,* VIII.

178. 　O joy ! that in our embers
　　　Is something that doth live,
　　　That nature yet remembers
　　　What was so fugitive !
　　The thought of our past years in me doth breed
　　Perpetual benediction.
(1803-6)　　—*Ode. Intimations of Immortality,* IX.

179. 　　Those obstinate questionings
　　　Of sense and outward things,
　　　Fallings from us, vanishings ;
　　　Blank misgivings of a Creature
　　Moving about in worlds not realised,
　　High instincts before which our mortal Nature
　　Did tremble like a guilty thing surprised.
(1803-6)　　—*Ode. Intimations of Immortality,* IX.

180. Our noisy years seem moments in the being
　　Of the eternal Silence.
(1803-6)　　—*Ode. Intimations of Immortality,* IX.

181.   Truths that wake
    To perish never.
(1803-6)   —*Ode. Intimations of Immortality*, IX.

182.   Though inland far we be,
    Our souls have sight of that immortal sea
        Which brought us hither.
(1803-6)   —*Ode. Intimations of Immortality*, IX.

183. In years that bring the philosophic mind.
(1803-6)   —*Ode. Intimations of Immortality*, X.

184. The Clouds that gather round the setting Sun
    Do take a sober colouring from an eye
    That hath kept watch o'er man's mortality.
            —*Ode. Intimations of Immortality*, XI.

185. To me the meanest flower that blows can give
    Thoughts that do often lie too deep for tears.
            —*Ode. Intimations of Immortality*, XI.

186. Two Voices are there ; one is of the sea,
    One of the mountains ; each a mighty Voice :
    In both from age to age thou didst rejoice,
    They were thy chosen music, Liberty !
(1807)   —*Thought of a Briton on the Subjugation
                of Switzerland.*
            (POEMS: TO LIBERTY, Pt. I., xii.)

187. The silent Heavens have goings on ;
    The stars have tasks.
(1807)   —*Gipsies* (1807 text).
            (POEMS: IMAGINATION, XVIII.)

188.   The music and the bloom
    And all the mighty ravishment of spring.
(1807)   —*To Lady Beaumont.*
            (MISC. SONNETS: Pt. II., xviii.)

189. Love had he found in huts where poor men lie ;
  His daily teachers had been woods and rills,
  The silence that is in the starry sky,
  The sleep that is among the lonely hills.
(1807) *—Song at the Feast of Brougham Castle.*
     (POEMS: IMAGINATION, XXV.)

190. The monumental pomp of age
  Was with this goodly Personage ;
  A stature undepressed in size,
  Unbent, which rather seemed to rise,
  In open victory o'er the weight
  Of seventy years, to loftier height.
(1807) *—The White Doe of Rylstone*, Canto III.

191.   Sing aloud
  Old songs, the precious music of the heart !
(1809)   *—Feelings of the Tyrolese.*
    (POEMS: TO LIBERTY, Pt. II., xi.)

192. Call not the royal Swede unfortunate,
  Who never did to Fortune bend the knee.
(1809) *—Call not the royal Swede unfortunate.*
    (POEMS: TO LIBERTY, Pt. II., xx.)

193. A few strong instincts and a few plain rules.
(1809) *—Alas ! what boots the long laborious quest.*
    (POEMS: TO LIBERTY, Pt. II., xii.)

194.   Unbounded is the might
  Of Martyrdom, and fortitude, and right.
(1810)   *—Ah ! where is Palafox ?*
    (POEMS: TO LIBERTY, Pt. II., xxiii.)

195. The vision and the faculty divine.
(1795-1814) *—The Excursion*, Book I., l. 80.

196.   Strongest minds
      Are often those of whom the noisy world
      Hears least.
(1795-1814)   —*The Excursion*, Book I., ll. 91-93.

197. Rapt into still communion that transcends
      The imperfect offices of prayer and praise.
                —*The Excursion*, Book I., ll. 215-216.

198.   That mighty orb of song,
      The divine Milton.
                —*The Excursion*, Book I., ll. 249-250.

199.   The good die first,
      And they whose hearts are dry as summer dust,
      Burn to the socket.
                —*The Excursion*, Book I., ll. 500-502.

200. This dull product of a scoffer's pen.
                —*The Excursion*, Book II., l. 483.

201.   Towers begirt
      With battlements that on their restless fronts
      Bore stars.
                —*The Excursion*, Book II., ll. 843-845.

202. Wisdom is oft-times nearer when we stoop
      Than when we soar.
                —*The Excursion*, Book III., ll. 231-232.

203. Pleased to have been, contented not to be.
                —*The Excursion*, Book III., l. 269.

204. Feelingly sweet is stillness after storm,
      Though under covert of the wormy ground!
                —*The Excursion*, Book III., ll. 280-281.

205. Wrongs unredressed, or insults unavenged.
                —*The Excursion*, Book III., l. 374.

206.   Monastic brotherhood, upon rock
Aërial.
      —*The Excursion*, Book III., ll. 393-394.

207. The intellectual power, through words and things,
Went sounding on, a dim and perilous way!
      —*The Excursion*, Book III., ll. 700-701.

208. Society became my glittering bride,
And airy hopes my children.
      — *The Excursion*, Book III., ll. 735-736.

209. By the storms of circumstance unshaken,
And subject neither to eclipse nor wane,
Duty exists.
      —*The Excursion*, Book IV., ll. 71-73.

210. And touch as gentle as the morning light.
      —*The Excursion*, Book IV., l. 89.

211. 'Tis, by comparison, an easy task
Earth to despise ; but, to converse with heaven—
This is not easy.
      —*The Excursion*, Book IV., ll. 130-132.

212. And the most difficult of tasks to *keep*
Heights which the soul is competent to gain.
      —*The Excursion*, Book IV., ll. 138-139.

213.   Rejoicing secretly
In the sublime attractions of the grave.
      —*The Excursion*, Book IV., ll. 237-238.

214. There is a luxury in self-dispraise ;
And inward self-disparagement affords
To meditative spleen a grateful feast.
      —*The Excursion*, Book IV., ll. 475-477.

215.   The mists
Flying, and rainy vapours, call out shapes
And phantoms from the crags and solid earth
As fast as a musician scatters sounds
Out of an instrument.
              —*The Excursion*, Book IV., ll. 521-525.

216. We live by Admiration, Hope, and Love ;
     And, even as these are well and wisely fixed,
     In dignity of being we ascend.
              —*The Excursion*, Book IV., ll. 763-765.

217.   Early he perceives,
Within himself, a measure and a rule,
Which to the sun of truth he can apply,
That shines for him, and shines for all mankind.
              —*The Excursion*, Book IV., ll. 807-810.

218.   Pan himself,
The simple shepherd's awe-inspiring God !
              —*The Excursion*, Book IV., ll. 910-11.

219.   I have seen
A curious child, who dwelt upon a tract
Of inland ground, applying to his ear
The convolutions of a smooth-lipped shell ;
To which, in silence hushed, his very soul
Listened intensely ; and his countenance soon
Brightened with joy ; for from within were heard
Murmurings, whereby the monitor expressed
Mysterious union with its native sea.
Even such a shell the universe itself
Is to the ear of Faith ; and there are times,
I doubt not, when to you it doth impart
Authentic tidings of invisible things ;
Of ebb and flow, and ever-during power ;
And central peace, subsisting at the heart
Of endless agitation.
              —*The Excursion*, Book IV., ll. 1132-1147.

219A. The glorious habit by which sense is made
    Subservient still to moral purposes,
    Auxiliar to divine.
       —*The Excursion*, Book IV., ll. 1246-1248.

220.   One in whom persuasion and belief
    Had ripened into faith, and faith become
    A passionate intuition.
       —*The Excursion*, Book IV., ll. 1293-1295.

221. Spires whose "silent finger points to heaven."
       —*The Excursion*, Book VI., l. 19.

222. Fictions in form, but in their substance truths.
       —*The Excursion*, Book VI., l. 545.

223. Ah! what a warning for a thoughtless man,
    Could field or grove, could any spot of earth,
    Show to his eye an image of the pangs
    Which it hath witnessed ; render back an echo
    Of the sad steps by which it hath been trod !
       —*The Excursion*, Book VI., ll. 806-810.

224. To a higher mark than song can reach
    Rose his pure eloquence. And when the stream
    Which overflowed the soul was passed away,
    A consciousness remained that it had left,
    Deposited upon the silent shore
    Of memory, images and precious thoughts,
    That shall not die, and cannot be destroyed.
       —*The Excursion*, Book VII., ll. 25-30.

225. Wisdom married to immortal verse.
       —*The Excursion*, Book VII., l. 536.

226. A Man he seems of cheerful yesterdays
    And confident to-morrows.
       —*The Excursion*, Book VII., ll. 557-558.

227. To every Form of being is assigned

         .   .   .

    An *active* Principle :—
    Spirit that knows no insulated spot,
    No chasm, no solitude ; from link to link
    It circulates, the Soul of all the worlds.
               —The Excursion, Book IX., ll. 1-15.

228. The mighty stream of tendency.*
               —The Excursion, Book IX., l. 87.

229. The primal duties shine aloft—like stars ;
    The charities that soothe, and heal, and bless
    Are scattered at the feet of man—like flowers.
         —The Excursion, Book IX., ll. 238-240.

230.   By happy chance we saw
    A two-fold image; on a grassy bank
    A snow-white ram, and in the crystal flood
    Another and the same !
         —The Excursion, Book IX., ll. 439-442.

231.   The Gods approve
    The depth, and not the tumult, of the soul.
(1814)   *—Laodamia.*
       (POEMS : IMAGINATION, XXXI.)

232.   Mightier far
    Than strength of nerve and sinew, or the sway
    Of magic potent over sun and star,
    Is love, though oft to agony distrest,
    And though his favourite seat be feeble woman's
       breast.
(1814)   *—Laodamia.*
       (POEMS : IMAGINATION, XXXI.)

---

* Familiarised to modern readers by Matthew Arnold's use of it in one
or more of his works.—ED.

233. Elysian beauty, melancholy grace,
  Brought from a pensive though a happy place.
(1814)   *—Laodamia.*
             (POEMS: IMAGINATION, XXXI.)

234. He spake of love, such love as Spirits feel
  In worlds whose course is equable and pure;
  No fears to beat away—no strife to heal—
  The past unsighed for, and the future sure.
(1814)   *—Laodamia.*
             (POEMS: IMAGINATION, XXXI.)

235. Of all that is most beauteous—imaged there
  In happier beauty; more pellucid streams,
  An ampler ether, a diviner air,
  And fields invested with purpureal gleams.
(1814)   *—Laodamia.*
             (POEMS: IMAGINATION, XXXI.)

236. Learn by a mortal yearning, to ascend—
  Seeking a higher object. Love was given,
  Encouraged, sanctioned, chiefly for that end;
  For this the passion to excess was driven—
  That self might be annulled.
(1814)   *—Laodamia.*
             (POEMS: IMAGINATION, XXXI.)

237. Yet tears to human suffering are due;
  And mortal hopes defeated and o'erthrown
  Are mourned by man, and not by man alone.
(1814)   *—Laodamia.*
             (POEMS: IMAGINATION, XXXI.)

238. What pure homage *then* did wait
     On Dion's virtues! while the lunar beam
     Of Plato's genius, from its lofty sphere,
     Fell round him in the grove of Academe,
     Softening their inbred dignity austere.
(1814)   —*Dion*, i.
              (POEMS: IMAGINATION, XXXII.)

239. But shapes that come not at an earthly call,
     Will not depart when mortal voices bid.
(1814)   —*Dion*, v.
              (POEMS: IMAGINATION, XXXII.)

240. Him only pleasure leads, and peace attends,
     Him, only him, the shield of Jove defends,
     Whose means are fair and spotless as his ends.
(1814)   —*Dion*, vi.
              (POEMS: IMAGINATION, XXXII.)

241.   Flaunting Summer—when he throws
     His soul into the briar-rose.
(1814)   —*The Brownie's Cell*, ix.
              (TOUR IN SCOTLAND, 1814, I.)

242. A cheerful life is what the Muses love,
     A soaring spirit is their prime delight.
(1814) —*From the dark chambers of dejection freed.*
              (MISCELLANEOUS SONNETS, Pt. II., iv.)

243. But thou, that didst appear so fair
     To fond imagination,
     Dost rival in the light of day
     Her delicate creation.
(1814)   —*Yarrow Visited.*
              (TOUR IN SCOTLAND, 1814, IV.)

244. Great is the glory, for the strife is hard!
(1815)   —*To B. R. Haydon.*
              (MISCELLANEOUS SONNETS, Pt. II., iii.)

245. Imagination lofty and refined:
   'Tis hers to pluck the amaranthine flower
   Of Faith, and round the Sufferer's temples bind
   Wreaths that endure affliction's heaviest shower,
   And do not shrink from sorrow's keenest wind.
(1815?)   *—Weak is the will of Man, his judgment*
                   blind.
      (MISCELLANEOUS SONNETS, Pt. I., xxxv.)

246. But [God's] most dreaded instrument,
   In working out a pure intent,
   Is Man arrayed for mutual slaughter,—
   Yea, Carnage is [his] daughter ! *
(1816)   *—Ode* (" Imagination—ne'er before
          content "), iv. 1816 *edn.*
      (POEMS: TO LIBERTY, Pt. II., xlv.)

247. For the power of hills is on thee.
(1816)   *—To ——, on her first ascent to the summit*
              of Helvellyn.
      (POEMS: IMAGINATION, XXXV.)

248. In youth we love the darksome lawn
   Brushed by the owlet's wing ;
   Then, Twilight is preferred to Dawn,
   And Autumn to the Spring.
   Sad fancies do we then affect,
   In luxury of disrespect
   To our own prodigal excess
   Of too familiar happiness.
(1817)   *—Ode to Lycoris*, ii.
      (POEMS: SENTIMENT, &c., XXV.)

---

  * Altered in after-editions to—
      But Man is thy most awful instrument,
      In working out a pure intent.

249. Still, as we nearer draw to life's dark goal,
  Be hopeful Spring the favourite of the Soul!
(1817)   —*Ode to Lycoris*, iii.
    (POEMS: SENTIMENT, &c., XXV.)

250. Oh! 'tis the *heart* that magnifies this life,
  Making a truth and beauty of her own.
(1817)   —*To Lycoris*, second Poem.
    (POEMS: SENTIMENT, &c., XXVI.)

251. Who comes not hither ne'er shall know
  How beautiful the world below.
(1817)   —*The Pass of Kirkstone*, iv.
    (POEMS: IMAGINATION, XXXIII.)

252. Beauty, for confiding youth,
  Those shocks of passion can prepare
  That kill the bloom before its time;
  And blanch, without the owner's crime,
  The most resplendent hair.
(1817) —*Lament of Mary Queen of Scots*, vi.
    (POEMS: AFFECTIONS, XX.)

253. What is youth?—a dancing billow,
  Winds behind, and rocks before!
(1818)   —*Inscriptions, Hermit's Cell*, i. (" Hopes,
     what are they ").
    (INSCRIPTIONS, X.)

254. From worlds not quickened by the sun
  A portion of the gift is won;
  An intermingling of Heaven's pomp is spread
  On ground which British shepherds tread!
(1818) —*Composed upon an Evening of extraordinary*
    splendour and beauty, ii.
    (EVENING VOLUNTARIES, IX.)

255. The sightless Milton, with his hair
    Around his placid temples curled ;
    And Shakspeare at his side—a freight,
    If clay could think and mind were weight,
    For him who bore the world !
(1820)   *— The Italian Itinerant, and the Swiss*
                   Goatherd, i.
        (TOUR ON CONTINENT, 1820, XXV.)

256. Meek Nature's evening comment on the shows
    That for oblivion take their daily birth
    From all the fuming vanities of Earth !
(1820)   *—Sky Prospect—from the Plain of France.*
        (TOUR ON CONTINENT, 1820, XXXIV.)

257. Turning, for them who pass, the common dust
    Of servile opportunity to gold.
(1822)   *—Desultory Stanzas.*

258. A Pastor such as Chaucer's verse pourtrays ;
    Such as the heaven-taught skill of Herbert drew ;
    And tender Goldsmith crowned with deathless
       praise !
(1820)   *—Seathwaite Chapel.*
        (RIVER DUDDON, XVIII.)

259. Still glides the Stream, and shall for ever glide ;
    The Form remains, the Function never dies ;
    While we, the brave, the mighty, and the wise,
    We men, who in our morn of youth defied
    The elements, must vanish ;—be it so !
    Enough, if something from our hands have power
    To live, and act, and serve the future hour ;
    And if, as toward the silent tomb we go,
    Through love, through hope, and faith's trans-
       cendent dower,
    We feel that we are greater than we know.
(1820)   *—After-thought.*
        (RIVER DUDDON, XXXIV.)

260. For all things are less dreadful than they seem.
(1821)   —*Ecclesiastical Sonnets*, Pt. I., vii. *Recovery*.

261.   Babylon,
    Learnèd and wise, hath perished utterly,
    Nor leaves her Speech one word to aid the sigh
    That would lament her.
(1821)   —*Ecclesiastical Sonnets*, Pt. I., xxv.
                          Missions and Travels.

262. As thou these ashes, little Brook ! wilt bear
    Into the Avon, Avon to the tide
    Of Severn, Severn to the narrow Seas,
    Into main Ocean they, this deed accurst
    An emblem yields to friends and enemies.
    How the bold Teacher's Doctrine, sanctified
    By truth, shall spread, throughout the world
        dispersed.
(1821)   —*Ecclesiastical Sonnets*, Pt. II., xvii.
                          Wickliffe.

263. Woman ! above all women glorified,
    Our tainted nature's solitary boast.
(1821)   —*Ecclesiastical Sonnets*, Pt. II., xxv.
                          The Virgin.

264. Partners in faith, and brothers in distress.
(1821)   *Ecclesiastical Sonnets*, Pt. II., xxxvii.
                  English Reformers in Exile.

265.   The feather, whence the pen
    Was shaped that traced the lives of these good
        men,
    Dropped from an Angel's wing.
(1821)   —*Ecclesiastical Sonnets*, Pt. III., v.
                      Walton's Book of Lives.

266. Meek Walton's heavenly memory.
(1821) *—Ecclesiastical Sonnets*, Pt. III., v.
Walton's Book of Lives.

267. Bodies fall by wild sword-law ;
But who would force the Soul, tilts with a straw
Against a Champion cased in adamant.
(1823 ?) *—Ecclesiastical Sonnets*, Pt. III.. vii.
Persecution of the Scottish Covenanters.

268. Truth fails not ; but her outward forms that bear
The longest date do melt like frosty rime,
That in the morning whitened hill and plain
And is no more ; drop like the tower sublime
Of yesterday, which royally did wear
His crown of weeds, but could not even sustain
Some casual shout that broke the silent air,
Or the unimaginable touch of Time.
(1821) *—Ecclesiastical Sonnets*, Pt. III., xxxiv.
Mutability.

269. Once ye were holy, ye are holy still ;
Your spirit freely let me drink, and live !
(1821) *—Ecclesiastical Sonnets*, Pt. III., xxxv.
Old Abbeys.

270. Give all thou canst ; high Heaven rejects the lore
Of nicely-calculated less or more.
(1821) *—Ecclesiastical Sonnets*, Pt. III., xliii.
Inside of King's College Chapel, Cambridge.

271. Where music dwells
Lingering—and wandering on as loth to die ;
Like thoughts whose very sweetness yieldeth proof
That they were born for immortality.
(1821) *—Ecclesiastical Sonnets*, Pt. III., xliii.
Inside of King's College Chapel, Cambridge.

272. They dreamt not of a perishable home
　　Who thus could build.
(1821)　　　　　　—*Ecclesiastical Sonnets*, Pt. III., xlv.
　　　　　　Inside of King's College Chapel, Cambridge.

273. With heart as calm as lakes that sleep,
　　In frosty moonlight glistening ;
　　Or mountain rivers, where they creep
　　Along a channel smooth and deep,
　　To their own far-off murmurs listening.
(1823)　　　　　　　　—*Memory.*
　　　　　　(POEMS : SENTIMENT, &c., XXIX.)

274. Shipwrecked, kindles on the coast
　　False fires, that others may be lost.
(1823)　　　　　　—*To the Lady Fleming*, vii.
　　　　　　(MISC. POEMS, XII.)

275. Soft is the music that would charm for ever ;
　　The flower of sweetest smell is shy and lowly.
(1823)　—*Not Love, not War, nor the tumultuous swell.*
　　　　　　(MISC. SONNETS, Pt. II., ix.)

276.　　　　　　　　To the solid ground
　　Of nature trusts the Mind that builds for aye.
(1823)　—*A volant Tribe of Bards on earth are found.*
　　　　　　(MISC. SONNETS, Pt. I., xxxiv.)

277. True beauty dwells in deep retreats,
　　Whose veil is unremoved
　　Till heart with heart in concord beats,
　　And the lover is beloved.
(1824)　　　　　　—*To*—— ("*Let other bards*")
　　　　　　(POEMS : AFFECTIONS, XV.)

278. Peace settles where the intellect is meek,
   And Love is dutiful in thought and deed.
(1824)   —*To* —— ("*O dearer far than light*").
            (POEMS: AFFECTIONS, XIX.)

279. No tongue is able to rehearse
   One measure, Orpheus! of thy verse;
   Musæus, stationed with his lyre
   Supreme among the Elysian quire,
   Is, for the dwellers upon earth
   Mute as a lark ere morning's birth.
(1824)   —*Written in a Blank leaf of Macpherson's
                  Ossian.*
       (POEMS: SUMMER TOUR, 1833, XXVII.)

280. But hushed be every thought that springs
   From out the bitterness of things.
(1824)   —*Elegiac Stanzas,* 1824 ("*O for a dirge*")
            (ELEGIAC PIECES, XIII.)

281. Type of the wise who soar, but never roam;
   True to the kindred points of Heaven and Home!
(1825)   —*To a Skylark* ("Ethereal minstrel").
            (POEMS: IMAGINATION, XXX.)

282. A Briton, even in love, should be
   A subject, not a slave!
(1826)   —*Ere with cold beads of midnight dew.*
            (POEMS: AFFECTIONS, X.)

283.   When a damp
   Fell round the path of Milton, in his hand
   The Thing * became a trumpet; whence he blew
   Soul-animating strains—alas, too few!
(1827)   —*Scorn not the Sonnet; Critic, you have
                  frowned.*
            (MISC. SONNETS, Pt. II., i.)

       * *I.e.,* the Sonnet.

284. But He is risen, a later star of dawn.
(1828)   —*A Morning Exercise.*
                    (POEMS: FANCY, I.)

285. Bright gem instinct with music, vocal spark.
(1828)   (Of the Lark)—*A Morning Exercise.*
                    (POEMS: FANCY, I.)

286.   When his * veering gait
     And every motion of his starry train
     Seem governed by a strain
     Of music, audible to him alone.
(1828)   —*The Triad.*
                    (POEMS: IMAGINATION, XL.)

287. Alas! how little can a moment show
     Of an eye where feeling plays
     In ten thousand dewy rays;
     A face o'er which a thousand shadows go!
(1828)   —*The Triad.*
                    (POEMS: IMAGINATION, XL.)

288. Blest be the song that brightens
     The blind man's gloom, exalts the veteran's
        mirth ;
     Unscorned the peasant's whistling breath, that
        lightens
     His duteous toil of furrowing the green earth.
(1828)   —*On the Power of Sound*, iv.
                    (POEMS: IMAGINATION, LI.)

289. The towering headlands, crowned with mist,
     Their feet among the billows, know
     That Ocean is a mighty harmonist.
(1828)   —*On the Power of Sound*, xii.
                    (POEMS: IMAGINATION, LI.)

* " The bird of Juno," *i.e.*, the Peacock.

290. Stern winter loves a dirge-like sound.
(1828)   —*On the Power of Sound,* xii.
                    (POEMS: IMAGINATION, LI.)

291.   No sea
    Swells like the bosom of a man set free ;
    A wilderness is rich with liberty.
(1829)   —*Liberty.*
                    (MISCELLANEOUS POEMS, III.)

292. The tear whose source I could not guess,
    The deep sigh that seemed fatherless.
(1830)   --*Presentiments.*
                    (POEMS: IMAGINATION, XLIV.)

293. The bosom-weight, your stubborn gift,
    That no philosophy can lift.
(1830)   —*Presentiments.*
                    (POEMS: IMAGINATION, XLIV.)

294. For busy thoughts the stream flowed on
            In foamy agitation ;
    And slept in many a crystal pool
            For quiet contemplation.
(1831)   —*Yarrow Revisited.*
                    (YARROW REVISITED, &c., I.)

295. The setting sun's pathetic light.
(1831)   —*On the Departure of Sir Walter Scott
                from Abbotsford, for Naples.*
                    (YARROW REVISITED, &c., II.)

296.   If rightly trained and bred,
    Humanity is humble, finds no spot
    Which her Heaven-guided feet refuse to tread.
(1831)   —*Highland Hut.*
                    (YARROW REVISITED, &c., XIV.)

297. Memory, like sleep, hath powers which dreams
    obey,
    Dreams, vivid dreams, that are not fugitive:
    How little that she cherishes is lost!
(1831)   *—Bothwell Castle.*
          (YARROW REVISITED, &c., XVIII.)

298. Beneath stern mountains many a soft vale lies,
    And lofty springs give birth to lowly streams.
(1833)   *—On the Frith of Clyde.*
    (POEMS: SUMMER TOUR, 1833, XXIV.)

299. Myriads of daisies have shone forth in flower
    Near the lark's nest, and in their natural hour
    Have passed away; less happy than the One
    That, by the unwilling ploughshare, died to prove
    The tender charm of poetry and love.
(1833)   *—" There!" said a Stripling, pointing with
                    meet pride.*
    (POEMS: SUMMER TOUR, 1833, XXXVII.)

300. Small service is true service while it lasts.
    Of humblest Friends, bright Creature! scorn not
    one;
    The Daisy by the shadow that it casts,
    Protects the lingering dew-drop from the Sun.
(1834)   *—To a Child. Written in her album.*
    (MISCELLANEOUS POEMS: XVII.)

301. Since every mortal power of Coleridge
    Was frozen at its marvellous source;
    The rapt One, of the godlike forehead,
    The heaven-eyed creature sleeps in earth:
    And Lamb, the frolic and the gentle,
    Has vanished from his lonely hearth.

Like clouds that rake the mountain-summits,
Or waves that own no curbing hand,
How fast has brother followed brother,
From sunshine to the sunless land.
(1835)   —*Effusion upon the death of James Hogg.*
(ELEGIAC PIECES, XVI.)

302. How does the Meadow-flower its bloom unfold?
Because the lovely little flower is free
Down to its root, and, in that freedom, bold.
(1842)   —*A Poet!*—*He hath put his heart to school.*
(MISCELLANEOUS SONNETS, Pt. III., xxxvii.)

303. A soft eye-music of slow-waving boughs.
(1842)   —*Airey-force Valley.*
(POEMS: IMAGINATION, IV.)

304. Minds that have nothing to confer
Find little to perceive.
(1845)   — *Yes! thou art fair.*
(POEMS: AFFECTIONS, XVI.)

305. That to this mountain-daisy's self were known
The beauty of its star-shaped shadow, thrown
On the smooth surface of this naked stone!
(1845)   —*So fair, so sweet, withal so sensitive.*
(POEMS: SENTIMENT, &c., XLII)

INDEX TO FAMILIAR
QUOTATIONS.

Index to Familiar Quotations.

L

A LIST OF THE BEST POEMS OF

WORDSWORTH.

" *To be recognised far and wide as a great Poet, to be possible and receivable as a Classic, Wordsworth needs to be relieved of a great deal of the poetical baggage which now encumbers him. . . . . What establishes in my opinion Wordsworth's superiority, is the great and ample body of powerful work which remains to him, even after all his inferior work has been cleared away.*"— From M. Arnold's Preface to his *Poems of Wordsworth.*

A List. of the Best Poems

OF

WILLIAM WORDSWORTH

ARRANGED (MAINLY) IN

CHRONOLOGICAL ORDER.

Note.—The following list of Wordsworth's best poems is arranged chronologically, the date of the composition of each piece being given on the left hand side of the page. The name of the Series to which they belong is also given, and the numbers refer always to the author's last editions, or editions issued subsequent to 1850 by Messrs Moxon, or Messrs Ward, Lock & Co. Asterisks are put to a number of titles; these indicate the pieces that are most likely to be enjoyed by those persons studying Wordsworth for the first time. The following abbreviations are used :—

Youth for *Poems written in Youth;*
Childhood for *Poems referring to the period of Childhood;*
Affections for *Poems founded on the Affections;*
Places for *Poems on the Naming of Places;*
Fancy for *Poems of the Fancy;*
Imagination for *Poems of the Imagination;*
Tour in Scotland for *Memorials of a Tour in Scotland;*
To Liberty for *Poems Dedicated to National Independence and Liberty;*
Tour on Continent for *Memorials of a Tour on the Continent;*
Tour in Italy for *Memorials of a Tour in Italy;*
Summer Tour 1833 for *Poems composed or suggested during a Tour in the Summer of* 1833;
Sentiment, &c. for *Poems of Sentiment and Reflection;*
Old Age for *Poems referring to the period of Old Age.*

COMPOSED

1824-1836. [Proem] " If thou indeed derive thy light from Heaven."

1786? Written in very early Youth.

(POEMS : YOUTH, II.)

COMPOSED

1789. *Remembrance of Collins.
>   (POEMS: YOUTH, V.)

1795. *Lines left upon a Seat in a Yew-tree.
>   (POEMS: YOUTH, VII.)

1797. *The Reverie of Poor Susan.
>   (POEMS: IMAGINATION, XIII.)

1798. A Night-Piece.
>   (POEMS: IMAGINATION, III.)

1798. *We are Seven.
>   (POEMS: CHILDHOOD, X.)

1798. Simon Lee, the Old Huntsman.
>   (POEMS: SENTIMENT, &c., VI.)

1798. Goody Blake and Harry Gill.
>   (MISC. POEMS, XV.)

1798. " Her eyes are wild, her head is bare."
>   (POEMS: AFFECTIONS, XXXVIII.)

1798. *Lines written in Early Spring.
>   (POEMS: SENTIMENT, &c., III.)

1798. *To my Sister.
>   (POEMS: SENTIMENT, &c., V.)

1798. *Expostulation and Reply.
>   (POEMS: SENTIMENT, &c., I.)

1798. *The Tables Turned.
>   (POEMS: SENTIMENT, &c., II.)

COMPOSED

1798.   The Complaint of a Forsaken Indian Woman.
(POEMS: AFFECTIONS, XXI.)

1798.   *Lines composed a few miles above Tintern Abbey.
(POEMS: IMAGINATION, XXVI.)

1798.   *The old Cumberland Beggar.
(POEMS: OLD AGE, I.)

1798.   Animal tranquillity and Decay.
(POEMS: OLD AGE, V.)

1798.   Peter Bell.
Latter half of Prologue, and from Stanza 8 to "Against the wind and open sky" of Part first.

1799.   The Simplon Pass.
(POEMS: IMAGINATION, VII.)

1799.   *Influence of Natural Objects.
(POEMS: CHILDHOOD, XVI.)

1799.   *"There was a Boy."
(POEMS: IMAGINATION, I.)

1799.   *Nutting.
(POEMS: IMAGINATION, VI.)

1799.   *"She dwelt among the untrodden ways."
(POEMS: AFFECTIONS, VIII.)

1799.   "I travelled among unknown men."
(POEMS: AFFECTIONS, IX.)

COMPILED

1799. *" Three years she grew in sun and shower."
             (POEMS : IMAGINATION, X.)

1799. "A Slumber did my Spirit seal."
             (POEMS : IMAGINATION, XI.)

1799. *A Poet's Epitaph.
             (POEMS : SENTIMENT, &c, VIII.)

1799. *Matthew.
             (POEMS : SENTIMENT, &c., X.)

1799. *The Two April Mornings.
             (POEMS : SENTIMENT, &c., XI.)

1799. *The Fountain.
             (POEMS : SENTIMENT, &c., XII.)

1799. The Danish Boy.
             (POEMS : FANCY, XXII.)

1799. *Lucy Gray.
             (POEMS : CHILDHOOD, IX.)

1799. Ruth.
             (POEMS : IMAGINATION, XXI.)

1800. The Brothers.
             (POEMS : AFFECTIONS, I.)

1800. *Michael.
             (POEMS : AFFECTIONS, XXXII.)

1800. The Idle Shepherd-Boys ; or, Dungeon-Ghyll
        Force.
             (POEMS : CHILDHOOD, XI.)

COMPOSED

1800. *The Pet-lamb.
        (POEMS: CHILDHOOD, XIV.) .

1800. "It was an April morning: fresh and clear."
        (POEMS: PLACES, I.)

1800. To Joanna.
        (POEMS: PLACES, II.)

1800. "There is an Eminence,—of these our hills."
        (POEMS: PLACES, III.)

1800. "A narrow girdle of rough stones and crags."
        (POEMS: PLACES, IV.)

1800. To M. H.
        (POEMS: PLACES, V.)

1800. *Hart-leap Well.
        (POEMS: IMAGINATION, XXIV.)

1800. "'Tis said that some have died for love."
        (POEMS: AFFECTIONS, XIII.)

1800. The Childless Father.
        (POEMS: AFFECTIONS, XXVIII.)

1800. Song for the Wandering Jew.
        (POEMS: FANCY, XXIII.)

1801. The Sparrow's Nest.
        (POEMS: CHILDHOOD, III.)

1801. "Pelion and Ossa flourish side by side."
        (MISC. SONNETS, Pt. I., v.)

1802. Beggars.
        (POEMS: IMAGINATION, XVIII.)
        M

COMPOSED
1817.   Sequel to the foregoing.
(POEMS : IMAGINATION, XIX.)

1802.   To a Butterfly ("Stay near me").
(POEMS : CHILDHOOD, II.)

1802.   *"My heart leaps up when I behold."
(POEMS : CHILDHOOD, I.)

1802.   *To the Cuckoo ("O blithe new comer").
(POEMS : IMAGINATION, II.)

1802.   "Among all lovely things my Love had
been."
(From POEMS, in 2 vols., 1807, Vol. I., p. 66.)

1802.   To a Butterfly ("I've watched you").
(POEMS : AFFECTIONS, III.)

1802.   *To the Small Celandine.
(POEMS : FANCY, XI.)

1802.   *To the Same Flower.
(POEMS : FANCY, XII.)

1802.   *Resolution and Independence ; or, the Leech-
Gatherer.
(POEMS : IMAGINATION, XXII.)

1802.   "I grieved for Buonapartè, with a vain."
(POEMS TO LIBERTY, Pt. I., iv.)

1802.   A Farewell.
(POEMS : AFFECTIONS, IV.)

1802.   *Composed upon Westminster Bridge, Sept. 3,
1802.
(MISC. SONNETS, Pt. II., xxxvi.)

COMPOSED
1802. *Composed by the Sea-side, near Calais.
          (POEMS: TO LIBERTY, Pt. I., i.)

1802. *" It is a beauteous Evening, calm and free."
          (MISC. SONNETS, Pt. I., xxx.)

1802. *On the Extinction of the Venetian Republic.
          (POEMS: TO LIBERTY, Pt. I., vii.)

1802. *To Toussaint L'Ouverture.
          (POEMS: TO LIBERTY, Pt. I., viii.)

1802. " Inland within a hollow vale I stood."
          (POEMS: TO LIBERTY, Pt. I., xi.)

1802. Written in London, Sept. 1802 ("O Friend!
          I know not which way I must look ").
          (POEMS: TO LIBERTY, Pt. I., xiii.)

1802. *London, 1802 ("Milton! thou shouldst be ").
          (POEMS: TO LIBERTY, Pt. I., xiv.)

1802. " Great men have been among us."
          (POEMS: TO LIBERTY, Pt. I., xv.)

1802. *" It is not to be thought of that the Flood."
          (POEMS: TO LIBERTY, Pt. I., xvi.)

1802. " When I have borne in Memory what has
          tamed."
          (POEMS: TO LIBERTY, Pt. I., xvii.)

1802. *Stanzas written in my pocket-copy of Thom-
          son's " Castle of Indolence."
          (POEMS: AFFECTIONS, V.)

1802. Composed after a journey across the Hamble-
       ton Hills, Yorkshire.
                   (MISC. SONNETS, Pt. II., xi.)

1806. "Those words were uttered as in pensive
       mood."
                   (MISC. SONNETS, Pt. II., xii.)

1802. *To the Daisy (" In youth from rock ").
                   (POEMS: FANCY, VII.)

1802. To the same Flower (" With little here to do.")
                   (POEMS: FANCY, VIII.)

1802. To the Daisy (" Bright Flower ! whose home ").
                (POEMS: SENTIMENT, &c., IX.)

1802. To H. C., Six years old.
                   (POEMS: CHILDHOOD, XV.)

1803. *The Green Linnet.
                   (POEMS: FANCY, IX.)

1803. *Yew-trees.
                   (POEMS: IMAGINATION, V.)

1803. "It is no Spirit who from heaven hath flown."
                (POEMS: IMAGINATION, XXVII.)

1803. At the Grave of Burns, 1803.
                (TOUR IN SCOTLAND, 1803, II.)

1803. Thoughts suggested the Day following, on the
       Banks of the Nith.
                (TOUR IN SCOTLAND, 1803, III.)

COMPOSED
1803. *In the Pass of Killicranky.
        (TOUR IN SCOTLAND, 1803, XIV.)

1803. Anticipation, October 1803.
        (POEMS: TO LIBERTY, Pt. I., xxvi.)

1803. The Farmer of Tilsbury Vale.
        (POEMS: OLD AGE, II.)

1804. *" She was a Phantom of Delight."
        (POEMS: IMAGINATION, VIII.)

1804. *" I wandered lonely as a cloud."
        (POEMS: IMAGINATION, XII.)

1804. *The Affliction of Margaret ——.
        (POEMS: AFFECTIONS, XXIV.)

1804. Address to my Infant Daughter, Dora, on
        being reminded that she was a month old
        that day, Sept. 16 [1804].
        (POEMS: FANCY, XXXII.)

1804. The Small Celandine (" There is a Flower ").
        (POEMS: OLD AGE, III.)

1805. Ode to Duty.
        (POEMS: SENTIMENT, &c., XIX.)

1805. *To a Skylark (" Up with me !").
        (POEMS: FANCY, X.)

1805. Fidelity.
        (POEMS: SENTIMENT, &c., XVIII.)

1805. Tribute to the Memory of the same Dog
        (" Lie here without a record ").
        (POEMS: SENTIMENT, &c., XVII.)

1805. To the Daisy ("Sweet Flower! belike one day ").
> (ELEGIAC PIECES, VII.)

1805. *Elegiac Stanzas, Suggested by a Picture of Peele Castle.
> (ELEGIAC PIECES, VI.)

1805. Elegiac Verses, in memory of my brother, John Wordsworth.
> (ELEGIAC PIECES, VIII.)

1805. *To a Young Lady, who had been reproached for taking long walks in the Country.
> (POEMS: IMAGINATION, XXXVI.)

1805. French Revolution ("Oh! pleasant exercise of hope and joy!").
> (POEMS: IMAGINATION, XXVIII.)

1799-1805. The Prelude—latter half of Book I.; latter part of paragraph commencing "I play the loiterer," of Book III.; the paragraph commencing "Yes, that heartless chase," of Book IV.; Book XII.; paragraph commencing "Oh! next to one dear state of bliss," and down to "Boundless, or guide into Eternity," of Book XIII.; first, second and third paragraphs of Book XIV.; and paragraph commencing "Child of my Parents!" of Book XIV.

1806. *Character of the Happy Warrior.
> (POEMS: SENTIMENT, &c., XXI.)

1806. A Complaint.
> (POEMS: AFFECTIONS, XIV.)

1806. *Stray Pleasures.
> (POEMS: FANCY, XXIV.)

1806. *Power of Music.
> (POEMS: IMAGINATION, XIV.)

1806. " Yes, it was the mountain Echo."
> (POEMS: IMAGINATION, XXIX.)

1806. *" Nuns fret not at their Convent's narrow room."
> (MISC. SONNETS, Pt. I., i.)

1806. *Personal Talk (four Sonnets).
> (POEMS: SENTIMENT, &c., XIII.)

1806. *Admonition.
> (MISC. SONNETS, Pt. I., ii.)

1806 " Beloved Vale !" I said, " When I shall·con."
> (MISC. SONNETS, Pt. I., iii.)

1806. " How sweet it is, when Mother Fancy rocks."
> (MISC. SONNETS, Pt. II., ii.)

1806. Composed by the side of Grasmere Lake.
> (POEMS: TO LIBERTY, Pt. II., v.)

1806. " With how sad steps, O Moon, thou climb'st the Sky."
> (MISC. SONNETS, Pt. II., xxiii.)

1806. *" The world is too much with us; late and soon."
> (MISC. SONNETS, Pt. I., xxxiii.)

1806. "With Ships the Sea was sprinkled far and nigh."
> (MISC. SONNETS, Pt. I., xxxii.)

1806. *To Sleep (three Sonnets):—
> 1. "O gentle sleep! do they belong to thee."
> 2. "A flock of Sheep that leisurely pass by."
> 3. "Fond words have oft been spoken to thee, Sleep!"
> (MISC. SONNETS, Pt. I., xii., xiii., xiv.)

1806. "Lines composed at Grasmere."
> (ELEGIAC PIECES, IX.)

1806. "Another year!—another deadly blow."
> (POEMS: TO LIBERTY, Pt. I., xxvii.)

1803-6. Ode. Intimations of Immortality from Recollections of Early Childhood.

1806. "Methought I saw the footsteps of a throne."
> (MISC. SONNETS, Pt. I., xxviii.)

1836. November, 1836 ("Even so for me a vision sanctified").
> (MISC. SONNETS, Pt. I., xxix.)

1807. *Thought of a Briton on the Subjugation of Switzerland.
> (POEMS: TO LIBERTY, Pt. I., xii.)

1807. Gipsies.
> (POEMS: IMAGINATION, XX.)

1807. *"O Nightingale! thou surely art."
> (POEMS: IMAGINATION, IX.)

COMPOSED

1807. *To Lady Beaumont.
                    (MISC. SONNETS, Pt. II., xviii.)

1807. *Song at the Feast of Brougham Castle.
                    (POEMS : IMAGINATION, XXV.)

1807. The White Doe of Rylstone ; or, The Fate of
          the Nortons—
                    Dedication of ("In trellised shed"), and
                    first seven paragraphs of Canto I.

1807. The Force of Prayer; or, the Founding of
          Bolton Priory.
                    (POEMS : SENTIMENT, &c., XXII.)

1809. "O'er the wide earth, on mountain and on
          plain."
                    (POEMS : TO LIBERTY, Pt. II., xiv.)

1809. "Say, what is Honour ?—'Tis the finest sense."
                    (POEMS : TO LIBERTY, Pt. II., xvii.)

1809. "Brave Schill! by death delivered, take thy
          flight."
                    (POEMS : TO LIBERTY, Pt. II., xix.)

1810. "Even as a dragon's eye that feels the stress."
                    (MISC. SONNETS, Pt. II., xxiv.)

1810. "Avaunt all specious pliancy of mind."
                    (POEMS : TO LIBERTY, Pt. II., xxviii.)

1811. Characteristics of a child three years old.
                    (POEMS : CHILDHOOD, V.)

1811. *Upon the sight of a beautiful picture.
                    (MISC. SONNETS, Pt. I., ix.)

COMPOSED

1795–1814.   The Excursion—
                1795–1798.   Book 1. The Wanderer.
                1798–1802.   Book II. The Solitary.
                1802–1814.   Book IV. Despondency
                Corrected.
                —————— Book IX. Discourse of
                the Wanderer, &c.

1814.   Laodamia.
                (POEMS: IMAGINATION, XXXI.)

1814.   Dion.
                (POEMS: IMAGINATION, XXXII.)

1814.   *Yarrow Visited.
                (TOUR IN SCOTLAND, 1814, IV.)

1815.   To B. R. Haydon.
                (MISC. SONNETS, Pt. II., iii.)

1815.   September 1815.
                (MISC. SONNETS, Pt. II., xiii.)

1815.   November 1.   (" How clear, how keen.")
                (MISC. SONNETS, Pt. II., xiv.)

1815.   "The Fairest, brightest, hues of Ether fade."
                (MISC. SONNETS, Pt. I., viii.)

1815.   "Weak is the Will of Man, his judgment
                blind."
                (MISC. SONNETS, Pt. I., xxxv.)

1815.   *" Hail, Twilight, sovereign of one peaceful
                hour ! "
                (MISC. SONNETS, Pt. II., xxii.)

1815.   " Brook ! whose Society the Poet seeks."
                (MISC. SONNETS, Pt. II., xxxi.)

1815.   "Surprised by joy—impatient as the Wind.'
                (MISC. SONNETS, Pt. I., xxvii.)

1816.   Invocation to the Earth.
                (ELEGIAC PIECES, XI.)

1816.   The French Army in Russia, 1812-13, 2nd
        Poem ("Ye Storms resound ").
                (POEMS: TO LIBERTY, Pt. II., xxxv.)

1816.   To ——, on her first ascent to the summit of
        Helvellyn.
                (POEMS: IMAGINATION, XXXV.)

1817.   Ode to Lycoris, May 1817.
                (POEMS: SENTIMENT, &c., XXV.)

1817.   To the Same.
                (POEMS: SENTIMENT, &c., XXVI.)

1817.   *The Longest Day.
                (POEMS: CHILDHOOD, XVII.)

1817.   The Pass of Kirkstone.
                (POEMS: IMAGINATION, XXXIII.)

1817.   Lament of Mary Queen of Scots.
                (POEMS: AFFECTIONS, XX.)

1818.   Inscriptions supposed to be found in and near
        a Hermit's Cell, 1818 :—
            I. "Hopes, what are they ? — Beads of
                Morning."
           II. Inscribed upon a Rock.
          III. "Hast thou seen, with flash incessant."
           IV. "Near the Spring of the Hermitage."
            V. "Not seldom, clad in radiant vest."
                (INSCRIPTIONS, X-XIV.)

1818. Composed upon an Evening of Extraordinary
Splendour and Beauty.
(EVENING VOLUNTARIES, IX.)

1819. Malham Cove.
(MISC. SONNETS, Pt. II., xxxiv.)

1819. Gordale.
(MISC. SONNETS, Pt. II., xxxv.)

1819. Written upon a Blank Leaf in " The Complete
Angler."
(MISC. SONNETS, Pt. I., xvi.)

1819. To a Snowdrop.
(MISC. SONNETS, Pt. II., xvi.)

1819. On seeing a tuft of Snowdrops in a Storm
("When haughty expectations prostrate lie ").
(MISC. SONNETS, Pt. II., xxi.)

1819. " Grief, thou hast lost an ever-ready friend."
(MISC. SONNETS, Pt. I., xix.)

1819. " I watch, and long have watched, with calm
regret."
(MISC. SONNETS, Pt. II., vi.)

1819. September 1819 (" The Sylvan Slopes ").
(POEMS: SENTIMENT, &c., XXVII.)

1819. Upon the Same Occasion (" Departing Summer hath assumed ").
(POEMS: SENTIMENT, &c., XXVIII.)

1820. " There is a little unpretending Rill.'
(MISC. SONNETS, Pt. I., vi.)

1820. "The Stars are Mansions built by Nature's hand."

(MISC. SONNETS, Pt. II., xxv.)

1820. To the Lady Mary Lowther.

(MISC. SONNETS, Pt. II., xvii.)

1820. Fish-women—On Landing at Calais.

(TOUR ON CONTINENT, 1820, I.)

1820. Brugès (Second Sonnet).

(TOUR ON CONTINENT, 1820, III.)

1820. Between Namur and Liege.

(TOUR ON CONTINENT, 1820, V.)

1820. Memorial, near the Outlet of the Lake of Thun.

(TOUR ON CONTINENT, 1820, XIII.)

1820. Composed in one of the Catholic Cantons.

(TOUR ON CONTINENT, 1820, XIV.)

1820. The Eclipse of the Sun, 1820.

(TOUR ON CONTINENT, 1820, XXVII.)

1820. Echo, upon the Gemmi.

(TOUR ON CONTINENT, 1820, XXXI.)

1820. Sky-prospect—from the Plain of France.

(TOUR ON CONTINENT, 1820, XXXIV.)

1820. To the Rev. Dr Wordsworth ("The Minstrels played their Christmas tune").

ECCLESIASTICAL SONNETS—*Continued.*—
   Part III. *xliii. Inside of King's College
                     Chapel, Cambridge.
         „   xliv. The Same.
         „   xlv. Continued.
         „   xlvi. Ejaculation.

1823. Memory.
                  (POEMS : SENTIMENT, &c., XXIX.)

1823. To the Lady Fleming (" Blest is this Isle ")
                  (MISCELLANEOUS POEMS, IX.)

1823. " A volant tribe of Bards on earth are found.
                  (MISC. SONNETS, Pt. I., xxxiv.)

1823. *" Not Love, not War, nor the tumultuous
         swell."
                  (MISC. SONNETS, Pt. II., ix.)

1824. *To ——, (" Let other Bards ").
                  (POEMS : AFFECTIONS, XV.)

1824. To ——, (" O dearer far than light ").
                  (POEMS : AFFECTIONS, XIX.)

1824. " How rich that forehead's calm expanse ! "
                  (POEMS : AFFECTIONS, XVII.)

1824. Elegiac Stanzas (" O for a dirge ! ").
                  (ELEGIAC PIECES, XIII.)

1825. *To a Skylark (" Ethereal minstrel ! ").
                  (POEMS : IMAGINATION, XXX.)

1826. " Ere with cold beads of midnight dew."
                  (POEMS : AFFECTIONS, X.)

1826. *Ode. Composed on May Morning.
    (POEMS: SENTIMENT, &c., XXXVIII.)

1826-34. *To May.
    (POEMS: SENTIMENT, &c., XXXIX.)

1826. The Pillar of Trajan.
    (TOUR IN ITALY, 1837, XXVIII.)

1827. Written in a blank leaf of Macpherson's Ossian.
    (SUMMER TOUR, 1833, XXVII.)

1827. To —— ("Happy the feeling from the bosom thrown ").
    (MISC. SONNETS. Dedication to ——.)

1827. *"Scorn not the Sonnet; Critic, you have frowned."
    (MISC. SONNETS, Pt. II., i.)

1827. Retirement.
    (MISC. SONNETS, Pt. II., viii.)

1827. "There is a pleasure in poetic pains."
    (MISC. SONNETS, Pt. II., xix.)

1827. To ——, in her seventieth year.
    (MISC. SONNETS, Pt. III., xvii.)

1828. A Morning Exercise.
    (POEMS: FANCY, I.)

1828. The Triad.
    (POEMS: IMAGINATION, XL.)

COMPOSED

1828. *The Wishing-gate.
          (POEMS : IMAGINATION, XLI.)

1828. The Wishing-gate Destroyed.
          (POEMS : IMAGINATION, XLII.)

1828. A Jewish Family.
          (POEMS : IMAGINATION, L.)

1828. On the Power of Sound.
          (POEMS : IMAGINATION, LI.)

1828. Incident at Bruges.
          (TOUR ON CONTINENT, 1820, IV.)

1829. " This lawn, a carpet all alive."
          (POEMS : SENTIMENT, &c., XXX.)

1829. Thought on the Seasons.
          (POEMS : SENTIMENT, &c., XXXIII.)

1830. Presentiments.
          (POEMS : IMAGINATION, XLIV.)

1830. " In these fair vales hath many a tree."
          (INSCRIPTIONS, VIII.)

1830. To the Author's Portrait.
          (MISC. SONNETS, Pt. III., xxiv.)

1831. The Primrose of the Rock.
          (POEMS : IMAGINATION, XLIII.)

1831. Yarrow Revisited.
          (YARROW REVISITED, &c., I.)

1833. Cave of Staffa. After the Crowd had departed.

> (SUMMER TOUR, 1833, XXIX.)

1833. Flowers on the top of the Pillars at the Entrance of the Cave.

> (SUMMER TOUR, 1833, XXXI.)

1833. *" ' There ! ' said a stripling, pointing with meet pride."

> (SUMMER TOUR, 1833, XXXVII.)

1833. " Tranquillity ! the sovereign aim wert thou."

> (SUMMER TOUR, 1833, XL.)

1833. *" Most sweet it is with unuplifted eyes."

> (SUMMER TOUR, 1833, XLVIII.)

1834. " Not in the lucid intervals of life."

> (EVENING VOLUNTARIES, IV.)

1834. " Soft as a cloud is yon blue Ridge."

> (EVENING VOLUNTARIES, VI.)

1834. The Labourer's Noonday Hymn.

> (POEMS : SENTIMENT, &c., XXXVII.)

1834. *To a Child.   Written in her Album.

> (MISC. POEMS, XVII.)

1835. *Extempore Effusion upon the death of James Hogg.

> (ELEGIAC PIECES, XVI.)

1835. " Why art thou silent?   Is thy love a plant."

> (MISC. SONNETS, Pt. III., xxv.)

COMPOSED

1837.   "Near Anio's stream I spied a gentle dove."
(TOUR IN ITALY, 1837, X.)

1838.   Composed on a May Morning, 1838.
(MISC. SONNETS, Pt. III., xxx.)

1841.   To a Painter.
(MISC. SONNETS, Pt. III., xxxii.)

1841.   On the same Subject (" Though I beheld ").
(MISC. SONNETS, Pt. III., xxxiii.)

1842. *"*A Poet !*   He hath put his heart to school."
(MISC. SONNETS, Pt. III., xxvii.)

1842.   "The most alluring clouds that mount the sky."
(MISC. SONNETS, Pt. III., xxviii.)

1842.   "Lo! where she stands fixed in a saint-like
trance."
(MISC. POEMS, Pt. III., xxxi.)

1842.   Airey-Force Valley.
(POEMS: IMAGINATION, IV.)

1842.   "Lyre! though such power do in thy magic
live."
(POEMS: IMAGINATION, XVII.)

1842.   To the Clouds.
(POEMS: IMAGINATION, XLVIII.)

1842.   "Wansfell! this household has a favoured lot."
(MISC. SONNETS, Pt. III., xlii.)

1845.   "Yes! thou art fair, yet be not moved."
(POEMS: AFFECTIONS, XVI.)

APPENDIX.

CANCELLED VERSION

OF

WORDSWORTH'S "ODE TO DUTY."

[This cancelled version of the *Ode to Duty* has never been given in any *variorum* edition of Wordsworth. It was discovered by me in a copy of the two volumes of *Poems* (1807) containing cancelled sheets, and which came into my hands early last year (1890). This is, in all probability, the first draft of the Poem, which the Poet thought necessary to revise while the above-named edition was in press. That the later versions are the best there can be no question: yet it may be regretted that its author did not retain (in his final text) the sixth stanza (lines 41-48). I append at the foot of these pages the version as given in the edition of 1807. Knowing that a cancelled version of so important a poem would be of interest to many Wordsworthians, I thought the present occasion a suitable one on which to present it.]

ODE TO DUTY.

THERE are who tread a blameless way
In purity, and love, and truth,
Though resting on no better stay
Than on the genial sense of youth:
Glad Hearts! without reproach or blot;
Who do the right, and know it not:

ODE TO DUTY.

(1807 VERSION.)

STERN Daughter of the Voice of God!
O Duty! if that name thou love
Who art a Light to guide, a Rod
To check the erring, and reprove;
Thou, who art victory and law
When empty terrors overawe;

May joy be theirs while life shall last
And may a genial sense remain, when youth is past.

Serene would be our days and bright;
And happy would our nature be;   10
If Love were an unerring light;
And Joy its own security.
And bless'd are they who in the main,
This creed, even now, do entertain,
Do in this spirit live; yet know   15
That Man hath other hopes; strength which elsewhere
    must grow.

I, loving freedom, and untried;
No sport of every random gust,
Yet being to myself a guide,
Too blindly have reposed my trust;   20
Resolv'd that nothing e'er should press
Upon my present happiness,
I shov'd unwelcome tasks away:
But henceforth I would serve; and strictly if I may.

From vain temptations dost set free;
From strife and from despair; a glorious ministry.

There are who ask not if thine eye
Be on them; who, in love and truth,
Where no misgiving is, rely
Upon the genial sense of youth:'
Glad Hearts! without reproach or blot;
Who do thy work, and know it not:
May joy be theirs while life shall last!
And Thou, if they should totter, teach them to stand fast!

Serene will be our days and bright,
And happy will our nature be,
When love is an unerring light,
And joy its own security.
And bless'd are they who in the main
This faith, even now, do entertain:
Live in the spirit of this creed;
Yet find that other strength, according to their need.

O Power of DUTY! sent from God   25
To enforce on earth His high behest,
And keep us faithful to the road
Which conscience hath pronounc'd the best:
Thou, who art Victory and Law
When empty terrors overawe;   30
From vain temptations dost set free,
From Strife, and from Despair, a glorious Ministry!

Through no disturbance of my soul,
Or strong compunction in me wrought,
I supplicate for thy controul;   35
But in the quietness of thought:
Me this uncharter'd freedom tires;
I feel the weight of chance desires:
My hopes no more must change their name;
I long for a repose which ever is the same.   40

Yet not the less would I throughout
Still act according to the voice

I, loving freedom, and untried;
No sport of every random gust,
Yet being to myself a guide,
Too blindly have reposed my trust :'
Resolved that nothing e'er should press
Upon my present happiness,
I shoved unwelcome tasks away;
But thee I now would serve more strictly, if I may.

Through no disturbance of my soul,
Or strong compunction in me wrought,
I supplicate for thy controul;
But in the quietness of thought:
Me this uncharter'd freedom tires;
I feel the weight of chance desires:
My hopes no more must change their name,
I long for a repose which ever is the same.

Yet not the less would I throughout
Still act according to the voice

Of my own wish; and feel past doubt
That my submissiveness was choice:
Not seeking in the school of pride   45
For " precepts over dignified,"
Denial and restraint I prize
No farther than they breed a second Will more wise.

Stern Lawgiver! yet thou dost wear
The Godhead's most benignant grace;   50
Nor know we anything so fair
As is the smile upon thy face;
Flowers laugh before thee on their beds;
And Fragrance in thy footing treads;
Thou dost preserve the Stars from wrong;   55
And the most ancient Heavens through Thee
          are fresh and strong.

To humbler functions, awful Power!
I call thee: I myself commend
Unto thy guidance from this hour;
Oh! let my weakness have an end!   60

Of my own wish; and feel past doubt
That my submissiveness was choice :
Not seeking in the school of pride
For " precepts over dignified,"
Denial and restraint I prize
No farther than they breed a second Will more wise.

Stern Lawgiver ! yet thou dost wear
The Godhead's most benignant grace ;
Nor know we anything so fair
As is the smile upon thy face ;
Flowers laugh before thee on their beds ;
And Fragrance in thy footing treads ;
Thou dost preserve the Stars from wrong ;
And the most ancient Heavens through Thee are
          fresh and strong.

To humbler functions, awful Power !
I call thee : I myself commend
Unto thy guidance from this hour ;
Oh ! let my weakness have an end !

Give unto me, made lowly wise,
The spirit of self-sacrifice ;
The confidence of reason give ;
And in the light of truth thy Bondman let me live !

Give unto me, made lowly wise,
The spirit of self-sacrifice ;
The confidence of reason give ;
And in the light of truth thy Bondman let me live !

The Birds of Wordsworth.

" *I heard a thousand blended notes. . . .*
The birds around me hopped and played,
Their thoughts I cannot measure:
But the least motion which they made
It seemed a thrill of pleasure."
—*Lines written in Early Spring.*

[The following is an Index to all the passages in Wordsworth's Poems descriptive of birds : I have not attempted to give the reference to every poem in which a bird is merely named—an index to the *descriptive* portions *only* being all that should be necessary for the Wordsworthian naturalist.]

CUCKOO. *On the Power of Sound*, II.
——— *The Cuckoo-Clock.*

DOR-HAWK. *The Waggoner*, Canto I., ll. 3-5.
DOVE. *A Morning Exercise.*
——— *To* ——— ("*Wait, prithee, wait!*")
——— "*Near Anio's stream, I spied a gentle Dove.*"
DUCK. *An Evening Walk.*

EAGLE. *Descriptive Sketches.*
——— *The Prelude*, Book VI., l. 535.
——— *The Recluse*, ll. 517-520.
——— *Rob Roy's Grave.*
——— *Vernal Ode*, V.
——— *The Excursion*, Book I., ll. 274-275; IV., ll. 397-401.
——— *Ecclesiastical Sonnets*, Pt. II., vii.
——— *Eagles. Composed at Dunollie Castle.*
——— *To the River Derwent.*
——— *On revisiting Dunolly Castle.*
——— *The Dunolly Eagle.*
——— *The Westmoreland Girl*, Pt II.

FALCON. *The Excursion*, Book III., ll. 2-4.
FIELDFARE. *The Excursion*, Book IV., l. 450.

HERON. *An Evening Walk.*
——— *Farewell Lines.* ("*High bliss*").

KINGFISHER ("Halcyon"). *Ode to Lycoris.*
——— *A Morning Exercise.*
KITE. *The Excursion*, Book I., ll. 564-565.
——— *Michael.*

LARK. *The Excursion*, Book IV., ll. 491-493.
——— *The Westmoreland Girl*, Pt. II.
LINNET. *The Tables Turned.*
——— *The Excursion*, Book I., l. 962.

LINNET. *Ecclesiastical Sonnets,* Pt. III., xxxiii.
———— *By the side of Rydal Mere.*
LINNET, THE GREEN.   *The Green Linnet.*
LINTWHITE (Linnet).   *Yarrow Unvisited.*

MAGPIE.   *The Idle Shepherd-Boys.*
MOCKING BIRD.   *The Excursion,* Book III., l. 946.
MUCCAWISS.   *The Excursion,* Book III., l. 947.

NIGHTINGALE.   *The Solitary Reaper.*
———— *" O Nightingale ! thou surely art."*
———— *The Excursion,* Book IV., l. 1167.
———— *A Morning Exercise.*
———— *June,* 1820.
———— *" 'Tis he whose yester-evening's high disdain."*
———— *By the side of Rydal Mere.*

OSTRICH.   *Song for the Wandering Jew.*
OWL.   *An Evening Walk.*
———— *The Idiot Boy.*
———— *" There was a Boy ;—ye knew him well."*
———— *The Prelude,* Book V., ll. 373-379.
———— *A Morning Exercise,* v. 1.
———— *" The leaves that rustled on this oak-crowned hill."*

PARROT.   *The Contrast.*
PEACOCK *"the bird of Juno."*   *The Triad.*
PIKE.   *An Evening Walk.*

RAVEN.   *The Idle Shepherd-Boys.*
———— *The Oak and the Broom.*
———— *Song for the Wandering Jew.*
———— *Fidelity.*
———— *The Recluse,* ll. 580-582.
———— *The Excursion,* Book IV., ll. 1178-1187.
———— *Epistle to Sir Geo. Beaumont.*

RAVEN.   *A Morning Exercise,* v. 1.
——— *Duddon Sonnets,* XVII.
REDBREAST.   *The Redbreast chasing the Butterfly.*
——— *The Prelude,* Book VII., ll. 18-31.
——— *The Excursion,* Book IV., ll. 385-387.
——— *Inscriptions* ("*Stranger! this hillock*").
——— *The Redbreast.*
——— *To a Redbreast*—(*In Sickness*).
——— *In the Woods of Rydal.*
——— *The Trossachs.*
——— "*I know an aged man constrained to dwell.*"
ROOK.   "*The Linnet's warble, sinking towards a close.*"

SAND-LARK.   *An Evening Walk.*
——— *The Idle Shepherd-Boys.*
SEAGULL.   *The Excursion,* Book VII., l. 753.
SEA-MEW.   *The Excursion,* Book IV., ll. 451-455.
SKYLARK.   *The Danish Boy.*
——— *Resolution and Independence,* V.
——— *To a Skylark* ("*Up with me!*").
——— ——— ("*Ethereal Minstrel*").
——— *A Morning Exercise.*
——— *Written in a blank leaf of Macpherson's Ossian.*
——— *Gold and Silver Fishes in a Vase.*
——— *Liberty.*
SNIPE.   *The Excursion,* Book VII., l. 752.
SPARROW.   *The Sparrow's Nest.*
——— *Ecclesiastical Sonnets,* Pt. I., xvi.
STOCK-DOVE.   *Resolution and Independence,* i.
——— "*O Nightingale! thou surely art.*"
STONE-CHAT.   *An Evening Walk.*
SWALLOW.   *The Excursion,* Book VII., l. 752.
——— *The Longest Day.*
——— *A Morning Exercise.*
SWAN.   *An Evening Walk.*

O

SWAN.   *Yarrow Unvisited.*
——— *The Recluse,* ll. 238-272.
——— *Vernal Ode,* V.
——— *Dion* (1820 version).
———-*" I heard (alas ! 'twas only in a dream)."*

THROSTLE.   *The Tables Turned.*
THRUSH.   *The Idle Shepherd-Boys.*
——— *"'Tis said; that some have died for love."*
——— *The Excursion,* Book VI., ll. 863-868.
——— *Ecclesiastical Sonnets,* Pt. III., xxxiii.
——— *" Hark ! 'tis the Thrush, undaunted, un-*
deprest."
——— *"'Tis he whose yester-evening's high disdain."*
——— *By the side of Rydal Mere.*
TURTLEDOVE.   *The Poet and the Caged Turtledove.*

WHIP-POOR-WILL.   *A Morning Exercise.*
WILD-DUCK.   *The Wild Duck's Nest.*
WOODLARK.   *The Excursion,* Book IV., ll. 1168-1169.
WREN.   *The Prelude,* Book II., ll. 118-128.
——— *The Excursion,* Book IV., ll. 383-389.
——— *Ecclesiastical Sonnets,* Pt. II., xxi.
——— *A Wren's Nest.*
——— *The Contrast.*

THE TREES, PLANTS, AND FLOWERS
OF WORDSWORTH.

" He spake of plants that hourly change
Their blossoms, through a boundless range
Of intermingling hues ;
With budding, fading, faded flowers
They stand the wonder of the bowers
From morn to evening dews."
—Ruth.

[The Prefatory Note to " The Birds of Wordsworth" also
applies to this Index to " The Trees," &c.]

ALDER. *Duddon Sonnets,* V.
AMARANTH. *"Weak is the will of man, his judgmen.*
blind."
ASH. *The Prelude,* Book VI., ll. 78-85.
———— *The Excursion,* Book VIII., l. 478.
———— *Duddon Sonnets,* V., XIII.
———— *Airey-Force Valley.*
ASPEN. *The Trosachs.*

BINDWEED. *The Excursion,* Book I., l. 728.
BIRCH. *An Evening Walk.*
———— *The Recluse,* ll. 562-569.
———— *Duddon Sonnets,* V., XXI.
BRAMBLE. *Ecclesiastical Sonnets,* Pt. II., xxi.
BROOM. *To Joanna (" Amid the smoke of cities ").*
———— *The Oak and the Broom.*
BUTTERCUP. *To the Small Celandine.*

CEDAR. *The Excursion,* Book VII., ll. 846-847.

CELANDINE, SMALL (Common Pilewort).   *To the Small Celandine.*

———— ———— *To the same.*

———— ———— *The Small Celandine* ("*There is a flower*").

CYPRESS.   *Ruth.*

———— *The Excursion*, Book VIII., l. 474.

———— *The Eclipse of the Sun*, 1820.

DAFFODIL.   *Foresight.*

———— "*I wandered lonely as a cloud.*"

DAISY.   *A Farewell.*

———— *The Prelude*, Book VII., l. 593.

———— *To the Daisy* ("*In youth from rock*").

———— ———— ("*With little here*").

———— ———— ("*Bright Flower*").

———— ———— ("*Sweet Flower*").

———— *To a child* ("*Small Service*").

———— "' *There !* ' *said a stripling, pointing with meet pride.*"

———— "*Soft as a cloud is yon blue ridge.*"

———— "*So fair, so sweet, withal so sensitive.*"

EGLANTINE.   "'*Tis said that some have died for love.*"

———— *The Waterfall and the Eglantine.*

ELM.   *The Prelude*, Book VI., ll. 73-76.

———— *The Excursion*, Book VII., ll. 620-622.

———— *Ecclesiastical Sonnets*, Pt. I., xxi.

EYEBRIGHT.   *Duddon Sonnets*, VI.

FERN, OSMUNDA.   "*A Narrow girdle of rough stones and crags.*"

FERN.   "*How often I have marked a plumy fern.*"

FIR.   "*When, to the attractions of the busy world.*"

———— *The Excursion*, Book VII., ll. 612-615 ; IX., ll. 499-502.

FURZE. *"It was an April morning; bright and clear."*

GOOSEBERRY. *The Excursion,* Book I., l. 456.
GRASS. *The Idiot Boy.*

HAREBELL. *The Prelude,* Book VI., ll. 221-223.
HAZEL. *Nutting.*
———— *"Mark the concentred hazels that enclose."*
HOLLY. *The Excursion,* Book III., l. 527 ; VIII., ll. 442-447.
HONEYSUCKLE. *The Excursion,* Book I., ll. 715-716 ; VI., ll. 1148-1150.

IVY. *The Excursion,* Book VIII., l. 480.
———— *To Lycoris* (second Poem).
———— *Ecclesiastical Sonnets,* Pt. I., xxi.

JASMINE. *Elegiac Stanzas (" O for a Dirge ").*
JONQUIL. *To a Snowdrop.*

LAUREL. *The River Duddon : Dedication to Rev. Dr Wordsworth.*
———— *The Russian Fugitive,* Pt. III.
———— *"Adieu, Rydalian Laurels ! that have grown."*
LILY. *Vaudracour and Julia.*
———— *The Recluse,* l. 591.
———— *The Excursion,* Book IX., l. 540.
———— *The Brownie's Cell,* ix.
———— *Poor Robin.*
———— *Elegiac Stanzas (" O for a dirge ").*
LILY OF THE VALLEY. *The Prelude,* Book II., l. 61.
———— *The Excursion,* Book IX., ll. 541-544.
LOVE-LIES-BLEEDING. *Love lies bleeding.*
———— *"Never enlivened with the liveliest ray."*

MAGNOLIA. *Ruth.*

PRIMROSE. *The Excursion*, Book I., ll. 815-816.
—— *Duddon Sonnets*, XXII.
—— *The Primrose of the Rock.*
—— *A Wren's Nest.*

ROSE. *To the Daisy* ("*In youth from rock*").
—— *The Prelude*, Book XI., l. 121.
—— *Ode : Intimations of Immortality*, II.
—— *The Excursion*, Book II., ll. 108-109.
—— *Elegiac Stanzas* (" *O for a dirge*").

SNOWDROP. *To a Snowdrop.*
—— *To* —— ("*Such age how beautiful !*").
—— *Sonnet : On Seeing a tuft of Snowdrops in a storm.*
STONE-CROP (YELLOW). *The Excursion*, Book I., ll. 716-719.
STRAWBERRY. *Foresight.*
—— *Duddon Sonnets*, VI.
SYCAMORE. *The Excursion*, Book V., ll. 460-461 ; VII., ll. 616-618 ; VIII., ll. 478-479.

THISTLE. "*A Narrow Girdle of rough stones and crags.*"
—— *The Excursion*, Book VI., ll. 688-690.
THORN. *The Thorn.*
THYME. *Duddon Sonnets*, VI.

VIOLET. " *She dwelt among the untrodden ways.*"
—— *To the Daisy* ("*In youth from rock*").
—— *Nutting.*
—— *The Excursion*, Book VII., l. 730.

WATER-LILY. *The Excursion*, Book V., ll. 567-569 ; IX., ll. 539-541.
WILD GERANIUM (" Poor Robin "). *Poor Robin.*
WILD-ROSE. "*How sweet it is when mother Fancy rocks.*"

WILD-ROSE. *The Brownie's Cell*, ix.
WILLOW. *An Evening Walk.*
WOODBINE. *Duddon Sonnets*, XXIV.

YEW. *Lines left upon a seat in a Yew-tree.*
———— *Yew-Trees.*
———— *The Excursion*, Book III., ll. 26-28 ; l. 527 ;
    VIII., l. 475.

ADDENDA.

DICTIONARY OF PERSONS :—
    I. BLACKETT (MISS). *To ——, on her ascent of Helvellyn.*
    CHAUCER (G.). *The River Duddon*, XVIII.
    GOLDSMITH (O.). ———— ———— ————
    HERBERT (GEO.). ———— ———— ————
    WORDSWORTH (CATHERINE). *"Surprised by joy—*
        impatient as the wind."
DICTIONARY OF PLACES :—
    I. FURNESS FELLS. *"Nuns fret not at their Convent's*
        narrow room."
    WHITEHAVEN. *By the Sea* (*" The Sun is couched "*).

ERRATA.

P. 88. ASIA, *Andes Mountains* transfer to AMERICA.
  119. No. 134, for *witout toil*, read *without toil.*
  139. No. 268, l. 2, for *to melt*, read *do melt.*
   „   „ 271. for *King' College*, read *King's College.*

AN INDEX

TO THE

ANIMAL AND VEGETABLE KINGDOMS

OF

WORDSWORTH

BY

J. R. TUTIN

(Compiler of " The Wordsworth Dictionary," etc.)

HULL

J. R. TUTIN

1892

PREFACE.

THE following indices to Wordsworth's descriptions of the animal and vegetable kingdoms will, the compiler hopes, be of substantial service to the student of the poet's verse which deals with nature. This feature of Wordsworth's poetry is the more interesting because of the unerring truthfulness of detail in all his delineations. Other great poets in their word-pictures of birds, trees, flowers, etc., have not unfrequently fallen into error—Wordsworth, I believe, rarely or never. This accuracy and truth can easily be accounted for from the fact that he was an "out-of-doors" poet. The bulk of his poetry was composed in the open air, and he never went to books (as Pope and some others did) to aid him in describing the "goings on" of the natural world. As has been lately remarked, he is incomparable as the poet of birds, and a large octavo volume ("The Birds of Wordsworth," by W. H. Wintringham) deals with Wordsworth's descriptions and allusions to birds. There is no need in this preface to furnish any examples of his unique way of describing the habits, etc., of animals, the appearances, etc., of plants and flowers. The indices will at once refer the reader to hundreds of examples.

In a volume entitled "The Wordsworth Dictionary," which was issued in 1891, I covered part of the ground covered in this pamphlet, having indexed all Wordsworth's chief descriptions of birds, trees, plants, and flowers. The present publication includes the *whole* of the animal and vegetable kingdoms, and I have now taken the pains to give the. *exact* references to the stanzas or lines. An edition of Wordsworth with the lines of the longer poems numbered has been a *desideratum* for years past. When Professor Dowden's edition of the poet's works—to be issued shortly—is ready, this long-felt want will be met, and the present index will be of greater service then than it is now, from the fact that single lines can be easily found. The arrangement into sections of the matter of this index will, I trust, facilitate reference; and if the following few pages prove an useful aid to the study of the great poet, I shall be well rewarded.

J. R. T.

HULL,
September 12th, 1892.

ANIMALS.

DORMOUSE.

The Borderers, Act IV., l. 117.

EMMET.

The Excursion, Book IV., ll. 430-431.

FAWN.

Lucy Gray, St. 3.
The Seven Sisters, St. 3.
"Three years she grew," St. 3.
To Enterprise, VI.
Characteristics of a child three years old, ll. 15-16
A Flower Garden, St. 2.
See also under DEER, STAG, DOE, ROE, *and* HART.

FOX.

The Excursion, Book VII., l. 745.
Ecclesiastical Sonnets, II., 21

GOAT.

The Excursion, Book IV., l. 884.
The Excursion, Book IX., ll. 564-565.

HARE.

An Evening Walk, l. 374.
The Childless Father, St. 1.
Lucy Gray, St. 3.
Incident characteristic of a favourite Dog.
Yarrow Unvisited, St. 2.
Resolution and Independence, II.-III.
Influence of Natural Objects, l. 37.
See also under LEVERET.

HART.

"Though narrow be that old man's cares."
Hart-leap Well.
See also under DOE, DEER, FAWN, *and* STAG.

HEIFER.

Descriptive Sketches, l. 360
The Recluse, ll. 524-531.
The Prelude, Book V., ll. 240-241 ; VIII., ll. 23-24.
Vernal Ode, I.
See also under COW, OX.

HORSE.

"Calm is all nature."
An Evening Walk, ll. 49-52, 132-133.
Influence of Natural Objects, ll. 31-32.
The Prelude, Book I., ll. 431-432.
Hart-leap Well.
To Enterprise, IV.
See also under COLT.

KITTEN.

The Kitten and Falling Leaves.
"Fly, some kind Harbinger," l. 6.
See also under CAT.

LAMB.

The Last of the Flock.
The Idle Shepherd-boys.
Anecdote for Fathers, St. 5.
The Pet-lamb.
The Kitten and Falling Leaves, ll. 76-79.
The Prelude, Book VIII., ll. 230-234.
Intimations of Immortality, St. II., III., X.
The Excursion, Book IV., ll. 410-412, VI., ll. 787-789, IX., ll. 170-171.
The Westmoreland Girl, Pt. I.
The Mother's Return, St. 11.
Sequel to "Beggars" ("Where are they,") l. 25.
Composed on a May Morning, 1838.
To Enterprise, VI.
See also under SHEEP.

LEVERET.

To the Daisy, (1st Poem) St. 10.
Maternal Grief, ll. 27-37.
See also under HARE.

LION.

Guilt and Sorrow, VIII.
Vernal Ode, V.
On the Power of Sound, II.

MASTIFF.

The Waggoner, Canto III., ll. 101-109.
See also under DOG.

MOLE.

Loving and Liking, l. 51.
The Excursion, Book IV., ll. 428-430.

MONKEY.

The Prelude, Book VII., l. 694.

MOUSE.

Loving and Liking, l. 39.
The Cottager to her Infant, St. 2.

OTTER.

The Brownie's Cell, VIII.

OX.

The Prelude, Book V., ll. 242-245.
See also under COW, HEIFER.

PANTHER.

Ruth, St. 7.

PONY.

The Danish Boy, IV.
The Idiot Boy.
See also under HORSE.

RABBIT.

Yarrow Unvisited, St. 2.

ROE.

Lucy Gray, St. 7.
Tintern Abbey.
The Brothers, l. 77.
The Dunolly Eagle.
See also under DEER, STAG, DOE, *and* HART.

SHEEP.

"When, to the attractions," ll. 27-32.
Lines left upon a Yew-tree seat, l. 20.
The Recluse, ll. 330-334.
The Excursion, Book IX., ll. 440-454.
Fragments of Verse.
Song for the Spinning Wheel, St. 2-3.
On the Power of Sound, II.
Inscriptions, V : "Rude is this edifice," ll. 23-26.
Inscriptions, XI., St. 1.
See also under LAMB.

SQUIRREL.

Peter Bell, Pt. III., St. 31.

STAG.

Hart-leap Well.
See also under DEER, FAWN, HART, *and* ROE.

WOLF.

The Prelude, Book I., ll. 541-543.
Composed during a storm.

BIRDS.

BELL-BIRD.

On the Power of Sound, II.

BIRD OF PARADISE.

Suggested by a Picture of a Bird of
Paradise
Upon seeing a coloured drawing of
a Bird of Paradise
A Morning Exercise, St. 6

BITTERN.

Evening Walk, l. 19

BLACKBIRD.

The Fountain, St. 10
The Prelude, Book VI., l. 760

BLUE-CAP.

The Kitten and Falling Leaves, ll.
63-75

BUZZARD.

Guilt and Sorrow, XII.
Address to a child, l. 15
Elegiac Verses in Memory of my
Brother, I., II.

COCK.

Evening Walk, ll. 146-155
Descriptive Sketches, l. 628
Guilt and Sorrow, XXXVII., XLII.
The Waggoner, Canto IV., l. 149
The Excursion, Book II., l. 344 ;
V., l. 800 ; VII., ll. 405-7
Ecclesiastical Sonnets, Pt. I., 22
Sonnet : To the Cuckoo
Near Rome, in sight of S. Peter's

COCKATOO.

The Dunolly Eagle

CORMORANT.

Ecclesiastical Sonnets, Pt. I., 3

CROW.

Guilt and Sorrow, V.

CUCKOO.

To the Cuckoo
"Yes ! it was the Mountain Echo "
Sonnet : To the Cuckoo
The Cuckoo at Laverna
The Solitary Reaper, St. 2
To Sleep ("A flock of Sheep")
The Excursion, Book II., ll. 346-
348 ; VII., l. 408
On the Power of Sound, II.
The Cuckoo-clock
"The Sun has long been set "
The Cuckoo and the Nightingale
The Excursion, Book VII., l. 408

DOR-HAWK.

The Waggoner, C. I., ll. 3-5
To S. H.
Evening Voluntaries, I., ll. 22-24

DOVE.

Loving and Liking, l. 50
The Prelude, Book I., ll. 140-143
Humanity, l. 25
To Sleep (" O gentle sleep ")
A Morning Exercise
To ——(" Wait, prithee ")
"Near Anio's stream I spied a
gentle dove"
See also under STOCK-DOVE *and*
TURTLE-DOVE

DUCK (Wild).

An Evening Walk, l. 281.
The Wild Duck's Nest.
The Blind Highland Boy, St. 38.

EAGLE.

Descriptive Sketches, ll. 68 ; 275-6 ; 334 ; 335 ; 358.
Song at feast of Brougham Castle, l. 120.
Loving and Liking, l. 50.
Liberty, ll. 37-40.
To Enterprise, I.
On the Power of Sound, XIII.
The Borderers, Act III., l. 381.
The Poet's Dream, St. 10.
The Blind Highland Boy, St. 10.
The Prelude, Book VI., l. 535.
The Recluse, ll. 517-520.
Rob Roy's Grave, St. 14.
Vernal Ode, V.
The Excursion, Book I., ll. 274-275 ; IV., ll. 397-401 ; VII., l. 748.
Ecclesiastical Sonnets, Pt. II., 7.
Eagles, composed at Dunolly Castle.
On revisiting Dunolly Castle.
The Dunolly Eagle.
To the River Derwent.
The Westmoreland Girl, Pt. II., St. 16.

FALCON.

The Excursion, Book III., ll. 2-4.

FIELDFARE.

The Excursion, Book IV., l. 450.

GLEAD.

The Excursion, Book VII., l. 751.

HAWK.

The Excursion, Book IX., ll. 491-494.
" Rest and be thankful."
Hints from the Mountains.
The Prelude, Book V., ll. 246-256.
The Excursion, Book V., l. 815.
See also under DOR-HAWK.

HERON.

An Evening Walk, ll. 285-286.
Farewell Lives (" High bliss.")
The Prelude, Book III., ll. 438-9.
Yarrow Unvisited, St. 2.

JAY.

Descriptive Sketches, l. 67.

KINGFISHER.

Ode to Lycoris, I.
A Morning Exercise, St. 6.

KITE.

An Evening Walk, ll. 90-91.
The Excursion, Book I., ll. 564-565.
Michael, ll. 11-12.

LARK.

The Borderers, Act I., l. 110.
The Prelude, Book XIV., ll. 382-387.
To the Daisy, St. 10.
Elegiac Stanzas ("Lulled by the sound,") St. 10.
Ecclesiastical Sonnets, Part II., 14.
The Excursion, Book IV., ll. 491-493.
The Westmoreland Girl, Part II., St. 16.
See also under SKYLARK, SAND-LARK, *and* WOODLARK.

LINNET.

Goody Blake and Harry Gill, St. 5.
The Longest Day, St. 5.
The Tables Turned, St. 3.
The Excursion, Book I., l. 962.
Ecclesiastical Sonnets, Part III., xxxiii.
By the Side of Rydal Mere, ll. 1-2.
See also under LINTWHITE.

LINNET (Green).

The Green Linnet.

LINTWHITE.

Yarrow Unvisited, St. 3.
See also under LINNET.

MAGPIE.

The Idle Shepherd-boys.
Resolution and Independence, I.
The Excursion, Book IV., l. 618.

MOCKING BIRD.

The Excursion, Book III., l. 946.

MUCCAWISS.

The Excursion, Book III., ll. 947-949.

NIGHTINGALE.

Descriptive Sketches, ll. 615-617.
To Enterprise, VI.
On the Power of Sound, XI.
To a Skylark, St. 2.
The Solitary Reaper, St. 2.
" O Nightingale ! thou surely art."
The Excursion, Book II., ll. 725-726 ; IV., l. 1167.
A Morning Exercise, St. 4.
June, 1820.
" 'Tis he whose yester-evening's high disdain."
By the Side of Rydal Mere, ll. 13-36

OSTRICH.

Song for the Wandering Jew, St. 6

OWL.

An Evening Walk, ll. 323-325, 375
The Idiot Boy, Sts. 1, 87, 89
" There was a boy—ye knew him well," ll. 10-16
The Prelude, Book V., ll. 373-379
A Morning Exercise, St. 2
" The leaves that rustled on this oak-crowned hill "
The Waggoner, Canto III.
Loving and Liking, l. 6
The Excursion, Book VI., l. 327
The Recluse, ll. 521-522
Ecclesiastical Sonnets, Pt. I., 22

PARROT.

The Prelude, Book VII., ll. 100-102
The Contrast

PEACOCK.

The White Doe of Rylstone, Canto IV., ll. 16-22
The Triad, ll. 46-52

PELICAN.

The Prelude, Book III., ll. 439-441

PLOVER.

The Russian Fugitive, Pt. IV., St. 2

POPINJAY.

The Prelude, Book III., l. 444

QUAIL.

French and Spanish Guerillas

RAVEN.

Guilt and Sorrow, IX., XII.
The Brothers, l. 276
The Idle Shepherd-boys, St. 1
The Oak and the Broom, St. 10
Song for the Wandering Jew, St. 5
Fidelity, St. 4
The Recluse, ll. 580-582
The Excursion, Book IV., ll. 519, 1178-1187
Epistle to Sir Geo. Beaumont, ll. 208-211
A Morning Exercise, St. 2
Duddon Sonnets, XVII.
" A little onward lend thy guiding hand," l. 32

INSECTS.

CATERPILLAR.

The Prelude; Book III., ll. 452-453.
The Excursion, Book VIII., l. 419

CRICKET.

The Cottager to her Infant, St. 2

FLY.

Written in Germany
Stanzas written in Thomson, St. I.
To Sleep ("O gentle sleep")
The Excursion, Book I., ll. 596-597

GLOW-WORM.

An Evening Walk, ll. 265-268
The Borderers, Act I., ll. 427-428

"Among all lovely things my love had been"
The Prelude, Book VII., ll. 32-38
The Waggoner, Canto I., ll. 7-8
The Pilgrim's Dream
Farewell Lines, ll. 17-24
The Pass of Kirkstone, I.
Ecclesiastical Sonnets, III., 5
The Primrose of the Rock, St. I.

GRASSHOPPER.

The Excursion, Book III., ll. 250-252

MOTH.

The Egyptian Maid, St. 37

NAUTILUS.

Liberty, ll. 35-36

SERPENTS AND REPTILES.

FROG.

Loving and Liking, ll. 15-18

LIZARD.

Ecclesiastical Sonnets, II., 21
Fort Fuentes, St. 2

LEECH.

Resolution and Independence, XV, XVIII.

NEWT.

Ecclesiastical Sonnets, II., 21

SLOW-WORM.

Inscriptions, VII. ("Stranger! this hillock,") l. 34

SNAIL.

Liberty, l. 72

SNAKE.

Fort Fuentes, St. 2
The American Lady's Love, XV.

TOAD.

Loving and Liking, ll. 7-10

VIPER.

Dion, IV.

WORM.

The Borderers, Act IV., ll. 147-149
The Prelude, Book VII., l. 39
The Excursion, Book IV., l. 426
In Lombardy
Liberty, ll. 73-74
See also under SLOW-WORM

FISHES.

DOLPHIN.

Ruth, St. 7
The Blind Highland Boy, St. 24

GOLD FISH.

Gold and Silver Fishes in a Vase
Liberty

HERRING.

Epistle to Sir G. H. Beaumont, ll. 75-76

MINNOW.

The Westmorland Girl, Pt. II., St. 7

PIKE.

An Evening Walk, l. 282
The Westmorland Girl, Pt. II., St. 7

SEA-HORSE.

Song for the Wandering Jew, St. 4

TROUT.

The Excursion, Book VIII., ll. 558-560

WHALE.

Liberty, ll. 33-34

TREES.

ALDER.

Duddon Sonnets, V.

APPLE.

Descriptive Sketches, l. 258
Yarrow Unvisited, St. 5

ASH.

The Prelude, Book IV., ll. 89-92 ; VI., ll. 78-85
The Excursion, Book VII., ll. 596-597
Duddon Sonnets, V., XIII.
Airey-Force Valley
See also under MOUNTAIN ASH

ASPEN.

An Evening Walk, l. 116
Descriptive Sketches, l. 625
The Trossachs

BIRCH.

An Evening Walk, ll. 104-105, 156
The Recluse, ll. 562-569
Duddon Sonnets, V., XXI.
The Excursion, Book VII., l. 696, 598-599

BRAMBLE.

Ecclesiastical Sonnets, Pt. II., xxi.

BRIAR.

An Evening Walk, l. 63

BROOM.

To Joanna ("Amid the smoke of cities,") ll. 38-40
The Oak and the Broom

CEDAR.

The White Doe of Rylstone, Canto IV., l. 55
Musings near Aquapendente, ll. 138-141
The Borderers, Act IV., l. 154
The Excursion, Book VII., ll. 846-847

SYCAMORE.

Guilt and Sorrow, XXV.
Tintern Abbey, l. 10
The Excursion, Book V., ll. 460-
461; VII., ll. 616-618; VIII.,
ll. 478-479

THORN.

The Thorn
See also under HAWTHORN

WILLOW.

An Evening Walk, l. 6
Written in "The Complete Angler"

YEW.

Lines left upon a seat in a Yew-tree
Yew-trees
The Excursion, Book III., ll. 26-
28; l. 527; VIII., l. 474-475

PLANTS AND FLOWERS.

BINDWEED.

The Excursion, Book I.; l. 728

BUTTERCUP.

To the small Celandine, St. 7

CARNATION.

The Excursion, Book I., ll. 724-
727

CELANDINE (Common Pile-wort).

To the Small Celandine
To the same
The Small Celandine ("There is a
flower")

CORN.

After visiting the field of Waterloo
Lines suggested by a Portrait, l. 58

DAFFODIL.

Foresight, St. 2
"I wandered lonely as a cloud"

DAISY.

A Farewell, St. 3
The Prelude, Book VII., l. 593
To the Daisy ("In youth from
rock,")
—— ("With little here")
—— ("Bright flower")
—— ("Sweet flower")
To a Child ("Small Service")
"'There!' said a Stripling, Point-
ing with meet Pride"
"Soft as a cloud is yon blue ridge"
ll. 8-11
"So fair, so sweet, withal so sen-
sitive," St. 2
Foresight
The Excursion, Book I., ll. 722-
723
Elegiac Musings ("With copious
eulogy,") ll. 48-49

DANDELION.

Vaudracour and Julia, ll. 136-141
"A narrow girdle of rough stones
and crags," ll. 17-25

EYEBRIGHT.

Duddon Sonnets, VI.

FERN (Osmunda).

" A narrow girdle of rough stones and crags," ll. 33-38

FERN.

" How often I have marked a plumy fern."
The Excursion, Book I., l. 462

FOXGLOVE.

An Evening Walk, l. 96
The Borderers, Act I., l. 403-406
The Prelude, Book VIII, ll. 393-406

GERANIUM.

See under WILD GERANIUM

GRASS.

The Idiot Boy, St. 57
Intimations of Immortality, X.
The Excursion, Book I., ll. 708-710
" This lawn, a carpet all alive," St. 3

HAREBELL.

The Prelude, Book VI., ll. 221-223, X., ll. 276-280

HEATHER.

The Borderers, Act III., l. 130

HONEYSUCKLE.

The Excursion, Book I., ll. 715-716, VI., ll. 1149-1151

HYACINTH.

Ecclesiastical Sonnets, Pt. I., 27

IVY.

The Prelude, Book VI., l. 82
Elegiac Musings (" With copious eulogy,") ll. 56-57
At Furness Abbey (" Here, where of havoc ")
The Excursion, Book VII., ll. 552-553, VIII., l. 480
To Lycoris (2nd Poem), ll. 22-23
Ecclesiastical Sonnets, Pt. I., 21

JASMINE.

Elegiac Stanzas (" O for a Dirge,") St. 7

JONQUIL.

To a Snowdrop

LICHEN.

The Thorn, I-II
An Evening Walk, l. 95

LILY.

An Evening Walk, l. 235
The White Doe of Rylstone, Canto I., l. 59
Humanity, ll. 23-24
Elegiac Stanzas (" O for a Dirge,") St. 8
Processions, St. 7
The Egyptian Maid, St. 13
Vaudracour and Julia, ll. 192-194
The Recluse, l. 591
The Excursion, Book IX., l. 540
The Brownie's Cell, IX.
Poor Robin, l. 2
Elegiac Stanzas (" O for a Dirge,") St. 8
See also under WATER-LILY *and* LILY OF THE VALLEY

LILY OF THE VALLEY.

An Evening Walk, l. 235
The Prelude, Book II., l. 61
The Excursion, Book IX., ll. 541-544

LOVE LIES BLEEDING.

Love Lies Bleeding
" Never enlivened with the liveliest ray "

MARIGOLD (Marsh).

A Farewell, St. 3

MOSS.

The Borderers, Act III., l. 161
The Excursion, Book I., l. 9 ; VII., l. 181
The River Duddon, III., l. 13
Ecclesiastical Sonnets, Pt. III., 40
The Thorn, IV.-V.

MOSS CAMPION.

Elegiac Verses ("The Sheep-boy Whistled,") II., V.-VI.

PANSY.

Intimations of Immortality, IV.

PINK.

The Excursion, Book VI., l. 1153

PERIWINKLE.

Lines Written in Early Spring, St. 3

PRIMROSE.

Lines written in Early Spring, St. 3
Peter Bell, Part I., St. 12
Foresight, St. 3
To the Small Celandine (first poem), St. 1

To the Small Celandine (second poem), St. 5
The Excursion, Book I., ll. 815-816
Duddon Sonnets, XXII.
The Primrose of the Rock
A Wren's Nest, Sts. 10, 11, 15, 17-18
A Farewell, St. 7
To May, St. 8

RAGWORT.

The Prelude, Book I., ll. 293-294

SNOWDROP.

" Who fancied what a pretty sight "
The Prelude, Book I., l. 616
Elegiac Stanzas (" O for a Dirge,") St. 7-8
To a Snowdrop
To —— (" Such age how beautiful !")
On seeing a Tuft of Snowdrops in Storm

SPEARGRASS.

The Excursion, Book I., ll. 943-946

STONECROP (Yellow).

The Excursion, Book I., ll. 716-719

STRAWBERRY.

Foresight, Sts. 1, 4
Duddon Sonnets, VI.

THISTLE.

" A narrow girdle of rough stones and crags," ll. 17-25
The Excursion, Book VI., ll. 688-690
The Warning, l. 108